GRIEF SURVIVOR

A Love Story

MARLA KANE POLK

COPYRIGHT 2020 MARLA KANE POLK

This work is licensed under a Creative Commons Attribution-Noncommercial-No Derivative Works 3.0 Unported License.

Attribution — You must attribute the work in the manner specified by the author or licensor (but not in any way that suggests that they endorse you or your use of the work).

Noncommercial — You may not use this work for commercial purposes.

No Derivative Works — You may not alter, transform, or build upon this work.

Inquiries about additional permissions should be directed to: marlapolkgriefsurvivor@gmail.com

Cover photo by Randy Polk
Author photo by Larry Kane
Back cover art by Savannah Cheatham
Cover Design by Pixel Studios
Edited by Kathryn F. Galán, Wynnpix Productions
www.marlakanepolk.com

PRINT ISBN 979-8-6509-9989-8

This book is for my future grandchildren, so they can get to know their grandfather

CONTENTS

INTRODUCTION 7
CHAPTER 1 9
CHAPTER 2 22
CHAPTER 3 32
CHAPTER 4 37
CHAPTER 5 39
CHAPTER 6 52
CHAPTER 7 62
CHAPTER 8 68
CHAPTER 9 75
CHAPTER 10 80
CHAPTER 11 88
CHAPTER 12 93
CHAPTER 13 100
CHAPTER 14 106
CHAPTER 15 112
CHAPTER 16 117
CHAPTER 17 122
CHAPTER 18 126
CHAPTER 19 135

CHAPTER 20 141
CHAPTER 21 147
CHAPTER 22 151
CHAPTER 23 158
EPILOGUE 162
THANK YOU 163
SITE REFERENCE 165
ABOUT THE AUTHOR 166

INTRODUCTION

IF YOU HAVE LOST a part of you then this book can comfort you. Know that you are not alone. If you find yourself laughing and crying simultaneously, then reading this will make you feel normal again. I never knew the kind of pain I felt was possible, yet it was only possible because of the type of love I experienced.

You will laugh and cry with me and end up with hope and joy that life goes on—differently, but on. You will have a stronger desire to love harder and more authentically. If, after you read this, you question how America grieves, then I have been successful. I am just an average woman who had the fate to love an extraordinary man. And I was lucky enough to realize it when he was alive.

My hope for you is that you will read this sweet story of the first year of my grief and know, if you had love and lost it, if I can survive, you can, too. If you still have your love with you, you will not take it for granted and will become better at your relationships, after reading this book.

CHAPTER 1

2013 STARTED OUT AS a great year. So, I never could have imagined that, before the year was over, I would not want to live or that every breath I took would be a struggle, a difficult decision, rather than an unconscious effort.

We ushered in the New Year in Hawaii. It was our last chance to spend a vacation together at my dad and stepmom's house in Kona, before they sold it and moved to the mainland. Justin, my blond, handsome, kind, and witty oldest son, and Wesley, the curly-headed life of the party who was also extremely good looking, were entertaining us with their general goofiness. Our kids took SCUBA lessons while we relaxed on the lanai, hiked, and planned our future as parents of young adults.

We had so much to look forward to. While our friends were dealing with empty-nest syndrome, my husband Randy and I were high-fiving each other that our hard work and love had paid off! Both of our sons were healthy and happy. Justin was going to graduate from Texas Tech University, and Wesley was doing well at A & M. We were feeling very free. Randy's property management company was providing income without our having to work too hard. We had put in our eighty-hour weeks when we were younger, working in our previous business, and now it was smooth sailing.

We heard stories from our friends about how sad they were, because they were now alone. We missed our kids (when we weren't vacationing with them in Hawaii), but we were definitely not miserable. We chose to give up a lot of our freedom to be around our kids when they were growing up, sacrificing many chances for adult activities to hang out with them. We'd loved it, but now it was our turn.

Randy had started his newest career as an artist sculpting and painting beautiful and highly creative pieces, most with a spiritual theme. I was helping run the Palm House, a neighborhood outreach center that helped at-risk women and children, and had started writing a novel. Since I was a little girl, I had wanted to write a book. Finally, I had created a story about a teenage girl who was homeless because her single mother had died suddenly.

We worked, we traveled, and we designed. It dawned on us we were alone in the house for the first time in twenty-two years, and we acted like newlyweds all over again. We always made each other laugh. He was the king of corny "Dad" puns. He understood my dry sense of humor and liked it. The only hint of storms approaching came in April 2013, when Randy began limping from the escalating pain in his hips. He managed it with ibuprofen, though, and wondered if all the time he'd spent playing football had been worth it.

Compassion is not my strong suit, so when he began to complain, I assured him he could wait to address his pain until after Justin's college graduation. So, he had an epidural to mask the pain and was told he needed both hips replaced, because they were bone on bone. He was only fifty-three years old, however, and no one could explain why this was happening so early and so dramatically.

The epidural bought us a little time to concentrate on Justin. We were very proud and excited when he graduated at the top of his engineering class that May 2013. Then we helped him move to Houston, though by then, Randy was in pain all the time, so mostly he was just there for moral support.

We'd helped Justin look for a place to live, but when we finally found one, he couldn't move in for a couple months, so he stayed with a friend's parents and commuted to his new "adult" job plus graduate school at Rice University. Justin and I were anxious at first, but Randy knew our son would put 100% into his work and school and be just fine. Randy was never a worrier. He had a fantastic balance of caring and not caring too much.

Finally, no matter how much I tried to delay the inevitable, it was time to address Randy's pain. The doctor suggested he go to Ft. Worth for the hip surgery, because he was afraid Randy might have a limp for the rest of his life if he had the procedure done in Abilene. The local surgeon only did posterior hip replacements, but our doctor believed Randy would have better success with an anterior hip replacement. Also, since Randy was so young and active, the doctor believed he shouldn't settle for anything less than total mobility, and so he referred us to his colleague. I will question that decision to go out of town for surgery for the rest of my life. If my husband had stayed in Abilene, would the outcome have been different?

The first surgery was scheduled for the end of August, 2013, after I went on an Alaskan cruise with Randy's mom, Carolynn, his aunt, and sisters Shelley and Susan. The trip was a girls' trip, a present from Randy's delightful eighty-five-year-old Aunt Norma. She had been taking us on a cruise once a year for years. Every year, Randy begged to go, and every year, she refused him, joking that we needed a vacation from him.

If I had to describe Randy with one word, it would be an adventurer and his pain was preventing him from his typical wanderlust. So, when good friends asked us to get on their boat in June of 2013 and take a trip on the Intercoastal Waterway, he immediately wanted to go. He wanted to squeeze this trip in before his surgery. Justin was settling in and getting to know Houston, and Wesley was working out of town as a camp counselor, so we were tempted. It didn't matter that he was in pain. He knew he would be in pain at home, also, and this was a place he had never been before. Looking ahead, once August came, we wouldn't be able to do much adventuring for at least the next half year, not with two hip replacement surgeries scheduled. And the thought of him being cooped up, recovering, was worse than the physical pain, so we agreed to go on the trip.

On the day after Memorial Day, I woke Randy up early, because we had to drop his black, hybrid SUV off for repair, because it kept stalling. Also, we had been excited about packing for the boat trip. Randy was unusually groggy and didn't want to get up, but finally he did and got in the shower. He never would do much without a shower.

After he toweled off, I went into the bathroom and found blood on the floor and counter. I asked him what had happened. Did he fall? He was acting funny and said he had passed out.

I insisted we go to the doctor or the ER. He didn't argue or act like his usual gentle macho self. He just agreed. He was dazed and confused—and not in a Led Zeppelin sort of way. He did say he felt fine, though. I called his doctor of twenty years and was told there were no appointments available, but that we could come to the lobby and wait. They would try to fit him in.

We waited, and I begged them to look at him. They were rude and busy and overworked, and they even asked if Randy had been drinking, because he was so out of it. He admitted to having a couple of drinks the night before, and then they pretty much wrote him off as being hung-over. They suggested, if I was so concerned, I take him across the street to the ER.

I have to live with the fact that I did not take him to the ER. Randy didn't see the point of a substantial medical bill, since our deductible was very high. Rationally, I know it wasn't my fault, as he was fully capable of making his own decisions and he wanted to wait at his own doctor's office. If I could turn back the clock, I would have insisted he go to the ER. Maybe I would have called an ambulance instead of driving him to the doctor. I know it wasn't logical to think this way, but logic comes from the front of the brain, while guilt, regret, and grief come from the middle of the brain, the emotional center, and I was operating emotionally; honestly, a little hysterically.

Finally, the PA saw him and said Randy had probably taken his blood pressure meds too close together late the night before and again early that day, which caused him to faint. He had had high blood pressure for about ten years that was controlled by medication. It was genetic; his sister Susan and father, Travis, also had it. Because he did hit his head on the way down, though, the doctor ordered an MRI, to rule out any head injury. So, Randy got the test, and we went home.

He kept telling me he felt fine, that it was his blood pressure meds and not to worry. Then the doctor called and said Randy needed to see a neurologist, because there was something on the MRI. It could be scar tissue from an old head injury, or he could have had a stroke. The earliest appointment available was at the beginning of July.

In typical Randy fashion, he took the news in stride, saying he was invincible, and insisted we go ahead with our plans for the boat trip. In fact, he took the mechanic's report far worse than the news from his doctor. His car could not be fixed without replacing the engine.

It was not worth it, so, even though he was in too much pain to drive, we had to buy a new car. We didn't get much for the trade-in, and it was a significant expense we hadn't planned on, but we had no choice. We bought a Jeep for him to drive when he recovered and parked it in the driveway.

We went on our brief boat trip and saw beautiful scenery, all a great distraction from Randy's pain. My anxiety about the upcoming neurologist appointment was more of an annoyance than his hips, though they hurt him a lot. As he waited to see the neurologist, he insisted he was not concerned at all and did not believe he had had a stroke. He was worried that the doctors might insist on delaying the hip-replacement surgery.

After what seemed like months, although it was only a few weeks, Randy met with the neurologist. First, the doctor asked him about any previous head injuries because there was a spot in his MRI. They were trying to figure out if it was scar tissue or a new issue. As a little boy, he had fallen out of a tree. Coupled with the fact that he knew the current president was Barack Obama, the neurologist said Randy did not have a stroke. The neurologist was friendly and funny. Randy tended to judge a doctor's competence based on whether or not he liked his attitude. If the neurologist had had a lousy bedside manner, Randy would have found another doctor. Randy truly believed you better have an excellent reason not to smile.

The doctor confirmed the spot on the brain scan must have been scar tissue, because Randy didn't have any clear signs of having had a stroke. However, to err on the side of caution, the doctor ordered a halter monitor test. Randy wore it for twenty-four hours, ruling out any possible cardiac reason for his passing out. His first hip replacement surgery was still on.

Randy had the choice of doing his pre-op tests with his doctor in Abilene, who could send the results over to the surgeon, or, he could have them done at the hospital in Ft. Worth. For convenience, we opted to do them in Abilene. That is decision number three that I have to live with. *Maybe* the other hospital would have found something during those tests. One of his pre-op tests was an echocardiogram, and he passed it and all the other tests that they ran.

In late June, Randy confessed to me he didn't think he could endure the pain in his hips for another eight weeks, until the surgery date in August. He was afraid to be alone while I went on the girl's cruise because of his loss of mobility and the increasing need for pain management. I told him I wouldn't leave him and would cancel the trip, even though I knew it would disappoint his family and waste his aunt's money. However, before I had the chance to cancel my trip, the surgeon called and said he had a cancellation and could get Randy in sooner.

The first surgery was now scheduled for July 17, his dad's birthday, and I was nervous. The night before we left for Ft. Worth, I admitted to Randy how scared I was that the surgery would not have a good outcome. The closer it got, the worse my "feeling" was. He assured me he knew he would live to be

100, and I believed him. We talked about what would happen when I died (first), and I got him to promise he would wait at least a year before getting remarried. I knew women would come out of the woodwork to help him in his time of need. I even had a few friends in mind for him.

Thankfully, I was wrong.

The first total hip replacement was a breeze. Justin and Wesley came to the hospital to see their dad, and he was doing really well; we left him to eat at our favorite Mexican restaurant, Joe T Garcia's. Our very close friends, Paul and Kathy, were with us in the hospital and joined us for lunch.

We came home three days later, and Randy did his physical therapy. The home health nurse who was monitoring his mandatory blood thinners noticed his heart rate was low and called the doctor. The doctor reduced his blood pressure meds, and none of us thought about the issue again. No one asked to see him or ordered any cardiac tests.

Randy rehabbed quickly. He was so excited to be pain-free in his new titanium hip that he could hardly wait for October 21, the date of his second hip replacement, so he would not hurt anymore and could get on with his life. He had a lot to explore.

In the middle of August, I left for the family cruise. Wesley agreed to stay with Randy for a day. Then Randy's dad, Travis, enthusiastically agreed to come to Abilene and "babysit" Randy after that, since he still was not supposed to drive, and I didn't feel comfortable leaving him alone even though he felt fine.

Then, on my first night away, before we had actually boarded the ship, I got a call from Wesley that Randy was recovering from another surgery. Wesley and Randy had decided to see the new Wolverine movie and sat in the row with a handrail in front, which made a great ottoman.

Unfortunately, Randy lifted his leg to watch the movie and realized it was a wrong and painful decision. He wasn't supposed to lift it higher than his knee. His artificial hip, which was not yet fully healed, came apart. In other words, his leg fell off, but his skin was still sutured, holding it in place.

When the movie was over—and not a minute before, because Randy insisted, he wanted to see the ending—Wesley and his friend, Patrick, carried Randy to the car and drove him to the ER.

In the ER, they tried putting the hip back in place without having to put him under general anesthesia but could not, hence the next surgery. By the time I heard about all this, Randy was at home feeling a little embarrassed for not following the doctor's orders about lifting his leg. He insisted I not come home from my trip, assuring me I should not worry.

I continued with my plans. Randy's dad arrived, and they enjoyed spending quality time together, playing the piano, eating out, and visiting. In West Texas that summer, we were in a drought, so they also drove to the lake north of Abilene, to see how low the water level was. On the way there, they drove around the brand-new veteran's cemetery just because it was there. Randy had not seen it yet.

The rest of the rehab time was uneventful, and the better Randy felt, the more he did and the more he looked forward to October 21. Since the second surgery was within ninety days of the first surgery, no pre-op tests were done. They approved the operation based on the previous results. I was not nervous this time, because the first hip replacement had gone so well.

On the day of the surgery, he was to arrive at the hospital at 6 AM that morning. He was congested and needed to clear his throat. This was not unusual; he'd had allergies his whole life. He told me not to inform the doctor he was congested, because he was afraid they would postpone the surgery, and he wanted it over with. He said he was really good at having surgery.

The first two hours I waited were easy. However, then another two hours passed, and I grew very nervous, because he'd been in and out of the first surgery in less than three hours. Eventually, they came out and told me the surgery had gone well, but he was having trouble in recovery. They were monitoring him closely, because he hadn't woken up in a reasonable amount of time.

Finally, they let me see him, and he was sitting up and drinking juice, joking around and in a great mood, as always. I immediately was put at ease. Friends came and stayed with me for the three days he was in the hospital, and it was kind of fun. We talked and laughed and worried about another friend who had taken a turn for the worse battling cancer. I told the kids not to travel to Ft. Worth from College Station and Houston, because their father was doing so well. They could see him at Thanksgiving.

On October 24, we were ready to go home to Abilene. No more hospitals or pain in the future, just recovery. While we waited for the doctor to release him, Randy was coughing. I found his nurse and told her about it. She said something about getting a chest X-ray, but she was swamped. She came into the room, listened to his chest, and decided all he needed was a Benadryl, which she gave him.

My dear friend of twenty-three years, Maria, came to drive us home. My close friend, Mandy, had been at the hospital, waiting and keeping us company for two days, but had left the day before. On the way home, we stopped and got lunch. Randy had his favorite meal—a cheeseburger and fried okra; he walked into the restaurant by himself and had a great appetite. During the entire two-and-a-half-hour drive home, he talked with Maria while she drove and I slept in the back seat. I hated driving in city traffic, and I hated going over overpasses, so Randy drove us most of the time. I was grateful Maria was there because I was so worn out. I think I finally gave myself permission to rest.

Even though Randy was the one who had been in constant pain, the last three months had taken a toll on me, too. I had to watch him in agony, and every time he winced or groaned or needed a pain pill, I felt it, also. He couldn't get comfortable, and for the first time in the thirty years I'd known him, he had not been happy. Seeing him like that had been horrible for me, the world's worst caregiver. So yes, I was so glad it was over, and we could go back to our routine, fun, active life.

When we got home, we both looked at the four days' worth of mail and greeted Bagel, our dog (we always named all our animals after carbohydrates). Then, Randy wanted to take a nap, because he didn't get much sleep in the hospital. The night before, the alarm attached to his finger had kept going off; each time, the nurse had come in and told him he needed to keep the monitor on his finger. He'd always assured the nurse it *had* been on his finger, but since his vitals were normal, nothing was done.

I lay down with him and slept for about thirty minutes. At 5 PM, I asked him if he wanted to sleep some more, and he said he did. I was glad he was getting some good and needed rest, which I figured would help with his healing process.

At about 6 PM, I ordered Chinese food and had it delivered. When it arrived, I looked in on Randy, but he was still asleep.

I didn't wake him to eat, because he'd had a big lunch and I figured he still needed the rest. At about 8 PM, I checked on him again, and he was still sleeping. My mother called, and I told her he was fine.

Finally, at 9:00 PM, after I'd watched the episode of *Grey's Anatomy* I had recorded, I decided to wake him to give him a pain pill.

I went into the bedroom, turned on the lamp, and told him to get up and walk a bit. He didn't respond. I shook him. Nothing. I had taken his cell phone and the house phone out of the bedroom, so he wouldn't be disturbed. Had he wanted to call for help but been unable to? I will never know.

When I couldn't wake him, I ran for the phone and called 911, screaming that my husband was unresponsive. I performed chest compressions for an endless amount of time while the operator assured me the paramedics were on the way. Finally, what seemed like twenty police officers and EMS personnel arrived all at once, telling me to get back. For a while, I sat on the chaise lounge in the bedroom, the same one the kids had slept on when they were little whenever they'd had a bad dream.

Then the police had to restrain me, because I wanted to go to Randy, and I was screaming. The first responders asked me if there was anyone who could take me to the hospital.

I called my friend Donna, who lived down the street. I went into the bathroom to put on clothes. I distinctly remember how complicated the process was of putting on my bra. I wanted so desperately to hurry, and yet I was moving in slow motion. The only reason I was even getting dressed was because someone had told me to do it. My own rational thought was gone and until then I had been only wearing a night shirt.

I came out of the bathroom and saw so many emergency medical personnel as well as police, I started screaming again. *Why were they still there? Why hadn't they left with Randy in the ambulance?* When I say screaming, I don't mean barking orders; I mean hysterical, guttural screams I had never heard before from myself or anyone else.

But Randy was en route to the hospital, the police assured me, and we left in Donna's car a minute or two behind the ambulance. Though Donna had lived in Abilene the same length of time I had, about twenty-five years, she took a wrong turn getting to the hospital. I didn't correct her because I was unable to speak.

CHAPTER 2

THE RECEPTIONIST IN THE ER wanted Randy's insurance information and medical history. She also told me the doctor was in with Randy. Friends started arriving. Donna had to make the dreadful call for my kids to come, because their dad might be dying. Our families were notified. Other people knew what to do, but I did not.

The doctor told me I was in shock. He took me to another room, where Randy was lying unconscious with so many machines and tubes connected to him. Candy was with me. It was *not* the scene you see in the movies, with me telling Randy how much I loved him and willing him to live. I was listening to the doctor give me information that I was unable to process as I stared at Randy. He could not speak or move, and I could not, either. I simply could not believe this was happening.

Randy was the strongest and happiest man I knew, but, though the doctor said they were able to get his heart started in the ambulance, there was no evidence of brain activity. He was too fragile to take for testing to determine the extent of the damage, so they were moving him to ICU, and I should call the family to say goodbye. The only hope I had was that I did believe in miracles. The doctor said the next twenty-four hours would tell the story.

We were moved upstairs to the ICU waiting room. I think it was about 3 AM by that point. I kept asking if I could see Randy; they kept saying no, they were trying to stabilize him. I kept telling everyone my kids weren't there yet, In other words, "You better keep him alive for them." By 5 AM, they arrived, and we were let in the room.

It was shocking how sick he looked. Less than ten hours earlier, I was talking to him, and he seemed fine. Now, we all spoke to him at his bedside, not really knowing if he could hear us or not. As the hours wore on, there were not any signs of life, yet I still clung to hope. I fantasized about Randy snapping out of it and telling beautiful stories about the other side.

Word got out, and many friends and family from all over the country crowded into the ICU waiting room. I do not know how they all got there so quickly from Chicago, Arizona, Kansas, Israel, Africa, and Hawaii, but by noon, I heard that there were more than 100 people waiting and praying and telling stories in the small waiting room in the hall.

The hospital staff gave us a private room for the immediate family. Paul and Kathy stood guard, so my kids and I, Randy's parents and siblings, and my parents and siblings could see him. Everyone loved Randy, and he loved everyone.

I seldom left his room, so I didn't see most of the people keeping vigil. My closest friends came in every once in a while, and told Randy who was out there praying for him. They also made a pact never to leave me. Not only did our friends and family come to support us, but the kids' coaches and teachers and friends also left their college towns and jobs to be there. Randy would have loved this much attention if they had been there to watch him play the trumpet or do a magic show or a rap. He would have been thrilled if they were there to see his artwork. But this kind of attention—I knew he hated it.

I just stood by his bed and listened to the monitor beep, not knowing if the noises were good news or bad news. A nurse came in to try to get Randy's wedding ring off his finger. He was so swollen that they thought they would need to cut it off. They brought another attendant who was able to remove it using some kind of oil, and she handed the ring to me. I then gave it to Justin, and he put it on his right hand. At that point, there was no way of knowing the ring would stay there for twenty-one months, until he switched it to his left hand on his wedding day.

Justin had optimistically brought his school project with him, thinking he would get it done while he waited. As the hours went by and Randy didn't wake up, he couldn't leave his father's bedside and concentrate, so he never did get his project done. Wesley went back and forth from his ICU vigil to checking on and giving reports to the hundreds of people young and old, family and friends in the waiting rooms.

About twenty-four hours after we arrived at the hospital, it occurred to me what was happening. Even though I'd talked to doctors and nurses and loved ones, and I made decisions and did what people told me to do, I was not really processing. I remember the moment I realized Randy was going to die.

I went into the room provided for the family, and I guess my friends Candy and Mandy, who were there with me, asked the others to leave. I lay down on something, the bed or chair or table—I can't say what, just that I was prone, and I screamed and screamed and cried hysterical, gut-wrenching sobs that were so foreign to me. These were not the sounds from soap operas, but animalistic. I remember my friends telling me to let it out. I had no choice; I could not keep it in any longer. That was the moment I knew that the best and most beautiful part of me was going to go away and I didn't know how to change it, that I would never be the same.

The doctors and especially the nurses started talking about how Randy's organs were failing, so if anyone came to talk to me about organ donation, I should know that wasn't an option. My older brother, Neil, who was the first out-of-town relative to arrive, told me to consider an autopsy. He wisely said, "If you get one, you don't have to read the results, but you can't go back and wish you had ordered one."

The hospital staff asked about a Do Not Resuscitate order: When he started crashing, which would happen soon, did I want to have them call a code and try to revive him? This was not making a decision to "pull the plug." Randy remained plugged into the ventilator, but they told me he would crash anyway. If I wanted, they could keep reviving him until it didn't work. The downside was, whenever a code was called, no one else could be in the room.

Did I trade my last moment with Randy for possibly another moment before his next-to-last moment that I could not be there for? At forty-nine years old, I did not have a reference manual for this. I did not know what to do, but it occurred to me that I had not called my best friend, who lived in Kansas City. Pam was in the medical field, so I called her and woke her up. A middle-of-the-night phone call is never good news, but with my call coupled with the desperation in my voice, she knew the situation was dire. She listened as I told her the facts and asked her what I should do, but we both knew that there was nothing I could do.

After I hung up, I managed to say to the intensivist to revive him once, but not over and over. It seemed like a good compromise, maybe one that would keep me from always thinking I should have done something different. I already had a list of regrets and decisions I would ruminate on for years to come. I have no idea why or how I thought of it, but that is what I told them to do.

The next several hours were filled with letting those who wanted to pray for a miracle pray, while the machines tracking Randy's vitals warned us that a miracle wasn't going to happen. I could not think of a downside to the prayers, but I myself was beyond hope. Those who wanted and needed to say goodbye were allowed to do so. When the nurse said Randy's kidneys were failing, my mother-in-law registered for the first time that this was very, fatally serious. I will never forget the look on her face when it changed from hope to grief.

Late in the afternoon of October 26, about forty hours after Randy arrived at the ER by ambulance, a code was called, and we were all ushered out of the room as they had warned us. I was back to stunned silence. After they revived him, someone told me I should go back into the room and say goodbye.

They gave me privacy. I just stared at Randy and realized there was nothing I needed to say that he didn't know. There were no regrets in that area. I knew he knew without a doubt that I loved him with my whole heart. I did not have to ask him to forgive me for anything I had said or done. There were no last-minute confessions, no estranged friends or relatives came to reconcile before it was too late. Randy knew his God, and he was the best example of a man dying at peace that I had ever heard of. It was the rest of us who did not have peace and would not have it for a long time.

I did ask Randy to wake up, but he didn't. Justin and Wesley, our sons, and Bryce, who was like a son, David, the pastor, and I gathered around Randy, holding hands. Many others watched on the other side of the glass. Justin started singing, "It is Well with my Soul," and we all joined in. We got about three words out before we were all crying as an accompaniment to David's singing. It was *not* well with my soul.

My father drove me home from the hospital. I did not even know where my kids or the other members of my family were, though I was told everyone had hotel rooms except my kids. I assumed all of the heartbroken found some place to sleep. Most of us had been awake for fifty hours.

I remember getting in the car in the hospital parking lot and looking up at the hospital, thinking that was the last place Randy was. I don't recall anything else until several hours later when, at about 10:00 PM, twenty-five of Wesley's and Justin's friends circled our bed, now my bed, and I asked them to tell me a bedtime story. I can't remember the details, but they all added a line to the story, one by one. These young people, the generation of the future, were trying and succeeding in taking care of me and I felt blessed.

His obituary read:

> *Randy "Mr. Fun" was never bored a day in his life. He had more hobbies, awards, certificates, and recognition than can be listed. He consistently gave all of his time and resources to those around him, and he exemplified the love of God and lived his life for His glory. His greatest accomplishment*

and the thing he enjoyed most in life was spending time with his family.

* * *

I came from a nonreligious Jewish home, and Randy grew up a Southern Baptist. We incorporated the best from both of our faiths into our daily lives.

Most of our family didn't understand what we believed or why, but we did and raised our kids in what Randy fondly called the Church of Marla. I wanted our unique perspectives represented, but, of course, Randy and I never talked about our funerals, because we were too young. Somehow, though, his funeral service was planned.

I remember sitting in the backyard, the same yard where we'd had endless parties with Randy being the best host, as we talked about what songs and verses I wanted, about who was to speak at the service? We decided to ask the men to wear Hawaiian shirts instead of suits, because that was Randy's typical ensemble.

We had a visitation the night before the memorial, and I do not know how I was capable of visiting with the thousand people who showed up to express their condolences.

One man had just come from the mall, where he'd been buying a Hawaiian shirt for the funeral when he'd bumped into another guy there to buy a Hawaiian shirt. They both looked at each other and said, "Randy Polk." The store clerk told them many men had been in that day looking for Hawaiian shirts for the same reason. We gave all the pallbearers one of Randy's many Hawaiian shirts to wear and to keep. To this day, our son

Wesley still wears Hawaiian shirts on Fridays, to memorialize his dad.

The funeral service was memorable and unique, just like Randy. It was part lūʻau, part art gallery, part sit-in, and it encompassed two different faiths. Our dear friend, Paul, insisted on putting together a video of Randy, to be watched at the funeral. Latimer, who was Randy's painting teacher and our friend, displayed his artwork in the foyer, so people could see it as they waited to be seated. There were at least one thousand people there, standing room only.

Mary Cathryn, Paul and Kathy's daughter and a dear family friend, sang, and Neil, my brother and the best man at our wedding, gave a stirring eulogy then asked people to donate in Randy's memory to expand the Palm House, a place we had put our hearts into for many years. Because there were not enough seats in the large sanctuary, all of Justin's and Wesley's friends sat on the floor in the front of the church. I looked from the picture of Randy on the easel next to the coffin to the kids on the floor and back to the image. At the moment in the church, when the kids were all there, I could feel Randy's presence in the room.

I had the thought that this was not so bad, that I could handle this. All I had to do was look at his picture, and I thought I would be fine. Again, I was very wrong. It would be a very long time until I was fine again. I was just experiencing a little grace, possibly arranged by Randy, to get me through the day.

I don't remember what my great friends Sam Peak and David Black said at the ceremony. Sam represented Judaism and David, Christianity, but people told me it was beautiful. It is weird that I don't remember what was said about the love of my life. But I do remember the funeral home attendant giving me particular orders, in a sympathetic yet bossy way, about where to sit and when to walk. I remember thinking who gives a crap. Who gives a crap was going to become my mantra and my outlook on life for a while.

The paper said there would be a private burial at the veteran's cemetery, to honor his military service, so only about 100 people were there. Randy was honored with *Taps* and a twenty-one-gun salute. I kept thinking Randy should be playing *Taps*, as he had many times before, instead of being the honoree.

After the funeral and burial, the limo dropped us back off at the church, and we had to leave Justin and Wesley there, because none of us had had the forethought to leave enough cars at the church. Someone gave a ride to someone else to pick up a car to go back for them. I was told my sons wrestled in the parking lot while they waited, as if they were nine and twelve years old, instead of nineteen and twenty-two. I guess they needed a reason to touch each other. Or maybe it was the spirit of their dad saying it was okay to have fun even now.

For a few days after the funeral, there were a great many people in and out of the house. All the people who were at the hospital now brought food and cards and words of sympathy. Randy's friends from high school and college, his relatives, his former employees, and co-workers paid their respects, and anybody he ever knew. Those first few days were a blur. Except for a couple of exceptions, the days following the funeral are thankfully lost.

I do remember all four of my siblings and their families all coming in and sitting at the dining room table. We tried to explain to Matt's son, my five-year-old nephew, the meaning of sarcasm. I also remember Wesley introducing me to many of his friends who had come down from his college.

And only two days after we buried him, I recall Justin sitting at the table and him saying something that made me laugh. Justin is quite funny, and we share a very dry sense of humor. As I laughed, I was surprised that I was able to laugh. I had really thought I would never laugh again. And so the healing had begun.

CHAPTER 3

IN THE DAYS AND WEEKS after the funeral, I did what people told me. Someone would bring me food, and I would eat it. Someone would come to see me, and I would see him or her. Mostly, I cried.

People went to the grocery store for me and went to the bank for me and did my laundry. Someone stayed at my house with me for fourteen continuous weeks. First, it was Justin, who needed to be at home to grieve, and was not ready to go back to Houston. He attended graduate school long distance and took a leave of absence from his engineering job. He stayed with me until we went to Arizona for Thanksgiving week.

Then, Wesley came home for a month during his Christmas break, and then Justin came back again. Finally, my mother came back for two weeks. It was really a great strategy to get me to stand on my own because, by the time everyone finally left, I was very ready to get people out of my house. I know this level of support is not typical, and most people do not have this kind of help, but everyone was especially concerned about me because I had known Randy since I was eighteen years old. I grew up with him. We worked together for twenty-five years, and we were married for twenty-seven. Very rarely were we apart for any length of time. On the last cruise I took before he died, my sister-in-law said she would love to stay on the cruise another week. I told her, even though Alaska was beautiful, I could not stand to be away from Randy that long because I missed him too much. It turned out to be a horrible prophecy of the parting that was to come.

I had so little energy that getting out of bed and showering was a great accomplishment. Writing thank-you notes to everyone who had supported my family and me was beyond my capability. I didn't give a damn about etiquette anymore, but I did want to do something unique for those special people who had helped my family so much.

I decided they would each get a beautiful photograph taken by Randy. For the past couple of years, he had been spending a lot of time at a place called Kirby Lake. Each day at sunset he would go for a walk and take pictures, if our schedule and the weather permitted. He always wanted to be alone on these walks; he was not even willing to take the dog. It was his time. Every photograph he took was of the western horizon viewed from the shore of the small lake at dusk. Because no two sunsets were alike, no two pictures were alike. He always seemed to get a different perspective.

As I stared at these photographs, I realized that in every photo, far on the distant horizon, was the hospital where he died. It was a weird, eerie reminder that there is always more to a picture than meets the eye. As Randy crouched to get the perfect image, was he aware of this distant symbol of his mortality? For each person or family member I knew would miss him, I picked a different sunset image to enlarge and frame. At the time, it was an engaging project to keep me busy, and over the years, it has brought me great comfort to walk into someone's home and see one of Randy's sunsets hanging on the wall. As if Randy is saying hi.

Randy's ability to make strangers friends with one hello is what drew us to the Palm House in the first place. The Palm House, a house in the inner city, was a safe haven for everyone who entered. Its primary purpose was to mentor at-risk women and children. Randy had spent a great deal of time there, making it a better place, building relationships with the kids, neighbors, and homeless whom we served. That is why it was not a hard decision to pick the Palm House to direct donations in Randy's memory.

The young elementary-age kids who attended the activities at the Palm House and who knew Randy were instructed to make me a sympathy card. Four days after he died, I received about thirty handwritten cards with little pictures of angels and notes in childish script about missing Randy while he was in heaven. The cards were poignant and hysterically funny because the cards were delivered the day before Halloween and each closed inappropriately with a joyful, "Happy Halloween!"

Randy would have loved them because Randy loved Halloween. Not in a Freddy Krueger, scary way, but as an excuse to have fun at someone else's expense kind of way. His favorite costume was one he put together himself: a wild wig and torn clothes with a hideous baby doll sitting on his shoulder. He liked to hide behind the steel door at work and scare each employee who walked in and then introduce him to the gruesome baby. I know this does not sound fun and is a little creepy, but Randy could pull it off. He had the most disarming grin and would never leave the scene of the crime without his victim laughing. The employee might scream and cuss him out, but there was always a laugh.

The first year we were in Abilene, which was 1989, Randy was very excited at the prospect of scaring the neighborhood kids. His first trick-or-treat customers were three little princesses, aged three through six, who had just emigrated from Israel and never experienced Halloween. When they rang the bell, Randy jumped out from behind the door with the hideous baby on his shoulder. The children started crying, and they ran away. Randy ran after them, because he felt so bad for making them cry. You can imagine how that went: with the evil man chasing them, the children screamed and ran faster. When they all reached their parents, Randy tried to calm the children by telling them he was sorry—but the only English the children had learned was "trick or treat" because they had just arrived in America the day before.

Realizing he had to act out his apology, Randy threw the baby on the ground with a thud, trying to show the screaming kids the baby wasn't real, and this abuse of the baby sent the children into full-blown panic. It took a long time to sort this out, but eventually, all was understood, and this family became our close friends. And this trick gone wrong did *not* make Randy learn his lesson—he kept "scaring" young and old alike.

My first Halloween without him, I did not answer the door. There were many people still keeping me company, so they might have put candy out... or not. I don't know. I was spending most of my time in bed, crying. When I accomplished anything beyond going to the bathroom, no matter how mundane, it felt like a huge accomplishment.

The first time I drove my car was a mistake. I had no way of knowing the toll trauma and grief would take on all my senses and my ability to react. Though I needed to be independent, and I didn't want to be a burden to anyone, so I drove to Candy and Geoff's for dinner. I had been there many, many times, yet I got lost driving the five miles. Eventually, Bagel and I made it. (I had asked if I could bring my dog.) I don't know what we had or whether I ate. What I do remember is Candy asking me if I would become her chef. She didn't enjoy cooking, even though she was good at it, and she knew I loved to cook—but no longer had anyone to cook for. I half-jokingly agreed to live with them and accept the position she had offered.

I did not end up living with them, of course, but I did end up cooking for them at their house every Monday. Picking the menu, then shopping and preparing the food gave me something creative and social to look forward to each week. I would go and talk about Randy and cry. After we ate, we watched disturbing television. First, it was *Breaking Bad*, then *Orange is the New Black*, and finally, *The Walking Dead*. It was very distracting. This was not my typical entertainment, but for one hour, I was grateful my life seemed better than the characters in the shows.

I myself was no longer typical. Now, I was a young widow and anything was on the table for viewing. I couldn't get enough of brutal, graphic television like *Dexter* and *Criminal Minds*. I compared my pain to these fictional victims and I thought things like, "Well, at least I haven't been buried alive lately..." It was really uplifting.

CHAPTER 4

AFTER THE FUNERAL, I announced to everyone that I would rescue dogs and cats and keep about ten animals at a time. This would keep me busy and give me a purpose,

I thought, I needed to find a new meaning for my life because I was no longer Randy's wife. Only a few hours after this declaration, Justin was sitting on the front porch when a beautiful male kitten walked up to him. He opened the door and yelled, "*Mom*! Here is your first cat!"

The little kitten walked right up to me and hopped in my lap in the midst of a room full of people. If I believed in reincarnation, this was Randy. It was a gray, longhaired male and very outgoing. He wasn't timid or scared, and he obviously had a connection to me.

Many hours were spent discussing what I should name my new pet. I already had a dog named Bagel and wanted to stay with the carbohydrates theme, so eventually, I settled on Strudel, because he was so sweet. A close friend suggested that I might want to see if anyone reported his or her cat missing, but I told her I didn't care I had just lost my husband; they could deal with losing a cat.

In 1986, the first year we were married, Randy adopted a white, long-haired Persian cat for me for my birthday. After much debate, because of his color, we named him Whitey Herzog after the St Louis Cardinals manager, and we called him Herzog. We loved that cat, and Randy spent a lot of time training him. He taught Herzog to do a front flip on command. The game was called "Get the Spider," and Randy would guide Herzog with a cat toy made from a stick with a fake, furry spider on its end. Eventually, Randy didn't need the stick. He could just say in a specific singsong cat voice, "Herzog, get the spider," and the cat would do a flip, jumping remarkably high. I had always heard you couldn't train a cat, but no one told Randy.

We joked about how we were practicing on cats before having kids. It seemed to be working. Herzog was growing and enjoying life in our little apartment in Topeka. Randy and I were having fun, acting like grown-ups most of the time. About six months into our feline parenthood, we made plans to go on vacation for a week. Randy talked about asking his friend and coworker to cat-sit. I talked about asking our neighbor to cat-sit.

I'm not proud to say we went to Texas for seven days, and when we came back, we realized, based on the state of the litter box and the empty food bowl, that no one had checked on Herzog. Thankfully, it appeared he had drunk water out of the toilet and survived. Cats are resilient, but we were not ready for children if we couldn't even take care of a cat.

We waited four more years to start our human family. I still leave the toilet lid open for the animals when I leave town—just in case.

CHAPTER 5

ON THE FOURTEENTH DAY after the day we died, I was sick. I had congestion and a cough and wanted to stay in bed. I was initially glad to be ill, because it gave me an excellent excuse to not get up, but I wasn't comfortable anywhere, especially in bed.

I fantasized that my cold was an incurable disease, that the pain of loss would be over soon, but I also faced the hard reality that I was on my own. Yes, I had friends who would come and bring soup in my hour of need, even take me to the doctor, and Justin was still at home, so I wasn't alone, yet I realized I would not be growing old with anyone, and we would not be taking care of each other. I thought of the symbiotic relationship between the sea anemone and clownfish. They could survive apart, but together they thrived. Did I have the strength?

Honestly, though, Randy had not been the best nurturer, when I was sick. I wasn't often ill, thankfully, but once, I did have pneumonia and was in bed for several days with fever and coughing. If you imagined him sitting by my bedside in my hour of need, feeding me chicken soup and fluffing my pillows, you didn't see Randy. Instead, he came every few hours wearing a mask and gloves, carrying a can of Lysol. From a distance, he tried to discern whether I needed to be transported to the hospital. Did I need anything? I could tell he hoped I didn't. I told him I was so lonely, but he did not give in and said he had to stay well for the kids who were not allowed to see me either, incidentally. It was quite a reunion when I was well enough to get up.

If you told Randy you didn't feel well, his first question was always, "Are you constipated?" He believed that covered most illnesses. His other healthcare tip was hydrogen peroxide, which he frequently put in his ears to listen to the bubbling. He knew most diseases could be cured with it and never went on a trip without a bottle of it. Randy was not the best nurse, even so, I knew he would always be there for me—until now. And this made me angry.

I wanted to wake up from this awful nightmare that had become my life. I wanted it to be like it was before. I missed Randy's giggle, and I wanted to be in his presence. I could not understand why, just because he was dead, I couldn't hear him or feel him. I was still crying for many hours a day. Usually, after a good cry, you feel better, cleansed. But I didn't. All I could imagine was endless crying in my future. I knew I hadn't scratched the surface of my despair, and I was terrified of what was to come.

The nights were the worst. Usually, Pam would call me. She was my lifeline and knew Randy as long as I did and loved him like the brother she never had. She lived out of town. She called me every night and asked me things like, "Did you shower today? Did you feed the dogs?" She would say hello then tell me something about nothing, like what her dog ate on their walk or how far she jogged. After that, I would cry for an hour, and she would listen. I am sure it was on speaker, and she was folding laundry or something, but that's not the point. She was there for me, a witness to my pain. She didn't try to fix the unfixable and didn't recite platitudes; she was just there for me. I now realize how important that was.

Everything was hard. I couldn't do any one thing for long. If I was crying, I wanted to stop. If I was working, I wanted to cry. If I was awake, I wanted to sleep. If I was sleeping, I would have bad dreams and wake up.

A frequent recurring nightmare was that Randy was alive, and I was so very happy to see him. I would tell him we were getting a second chance, that he could now go to the doctor, be healed, and not die. But he always refused to go. In my dream, I would go from great joy to great sadness. I woke up day after day only to realize he wasn't lying beside me in bed, that he was still gone. Over and over, I had to face the same reality. It was more than a year before I could wake up and, for a split second, forget before Randy's death crashed in on me again with fresh force. I was so tired all the time, tired from not sleeping, exhausted from emotional trauma, and worn out from trying to do Randy's job managing rental properties as well as my own job, doing the books for the rental properties. In addition to bookkeeping, I worked at the Palm House, the small nonprofit with the mission of helping vulnerable women and children. The Palm House was to become another lifeline.

For a while, I was useless. Though I did not help anyone during our service work at the Palm House, I did continue to show up. Most of the time, I cried while I was there, but for those few hours of my week, I had to be somewhere. Being self-employed had given me a great deal of freedom for a long time, but now that freedom felt like hours of aimless, solitary loneliness every week.

On Day 20, my friend Rebel, one of my lifelines, suggested I visit Wesley to spend some time with him and "celebrate" Randy's birthday. Rebel was my mom partner. For years, she would make sure I knew when the games and proms and tests were, because I would have trouble getting pertinent information, as a mother of boys. I helped raise her kids and she helped raise mine, giving each other a safe place to land when needed.

Wesley was very courageous, going back to school a couple days after the funeral, because he couldn't afford to miss class. So, Justin and Bagel and I took Rebel's advice and drove to visit Wesley at college, but the bits and pieces I remember about the weekend are sparse. Wesley, who had four housemates, arranged for me to stay at the house of his sweet then-girlfriend and now wife, Maddie. She shared it with girls named Madison and Madilyn, and they called it the "Mad House"; it was just a few houses down from his own. Wesley thought I would be more comfortable there, in a girl's house with my own space. The girls were away for the weekend so I went over there to sleep, but even with my newly prescribed sleeping pills, I could not stand it.

I hadn't been alone in twenty-seven years twenty days and, I was a wreck, so I went back to Wesley's and asked if I could stay in his room. He had to double up with one of the other boys, and I made everyone uncomfortable, but I didn't know what else to do. I lay on his bed and cried and cried.

Justin came in, and Wesley came in, but I was not to be consoled. I kept saying, "I don't think I can do this." I listened over and over to the last voicemail Randy left me. This was one of my lowest moments, turning to my kids for help when I should have been helping them.

I had to find a way out of this pit. I was not going to be a burden... but no matter how strong my will was, my grief was stronger. Wesley devised a plan for me to live with him and his four roommates and cook for them. They would get great food, and I wouldn't be lonely. The offer was appealing, but I had to go home and face my new reality.

Being there with all those college kids and seeing all their idealism and young love made me think of Randy and how we met, when we were in college. It was September 1982. He was wearing a T-shirt and gold, very short, polyester gym shorts. There is no other way to put it but to say he was beautiful. This was the era of Richard Simmons' and Jane Fonda's aerobics.

We were in an aerobics class of about two hundred women... and two men. I was in the back, as I usually was, both because I was habitually late and because I didn't want other people looking at me. I wanted a perfect view of this beautiful man's very muscular legs and broad shoulders. He had a beard, which I thought was very sexy, as some of my male friends were still wishing they could grow a decent beard. The first few weeks, I just looked at him to pass the time and get through the very physically tough hour. As time passed, I began to notice the smile that never left his face, even while grimacing during the grapevine step. His smile went from his sky-blue eyes to his mouth and back up to his eyes. He smiled so big he squinted.

As I settled into my new life as a freshman at college, I realized I wanted to dump my high school boyfriend. I should be going out with someone like this guy in my aerobics class, someone who was always happy, not the brooding, angry guy I had been settling for. Of course, at this point, I wasn't thinking of Randy as my boyfriend, let alone my husband. He was more a model of the perfect man.

Sometime after Thanksgiving, between leg warmers and Olivia Newton John's, "Physical," I started considering the possibility that Randy was gay. He was the most heterosexual-looking man I had ever seen, but why would he be in aerobics if he was straight? AIDS had just surfaced, and though Richard Simmons was the aerobics guru, men did not do women's dance classes in 1982—except for Randy Polk and the friend who came to class with him.

On the last day of the semester, I finally got up the nerve to talk to him, telling myself this was more about sociology than biology. I walked up to him and said, "Excuse me. You don't know me, but I want to ask you a personal question—Are you gay? I don't care or anything. Just wondering why are you in this class."

He laughed this great laugh that matched his smile and said, no, he just had to fill his schedule before graduating in a couple weeks, with a B.S. in geology. So, in one blow, there was good news—he wasn't gay, and lousy news—he was graduating. I said, "Okay, thanks," and walked away.

By the middle of January 1983, I'd spent a month at home for semester break and couldn't wait to get back to school. I was in one of the student cafeterias when I saw Randy Polk, although, at that point, I still didn't know his name. I approached him and asked, "What are you doing here? I thought you graduated."

He said, while smiling, "Sorry, do I know you?"

I told him we had met in aerobics, but he didn't remember me. He told me he had decided to get his M.B.A., so would be sticking around another couple of years. After that encounter, he did recognize me, and we looked for each other during that same time slot daily.

I still had never seen him in anything but a T-shirt and shorts. I can see him in my mind's eye at age twenty-three as clearly as I can see him at fifty-three, the age he was when he died. I think that's one thing about true love: you always see your loved one as he or she looked when you first fell in love. Maybe that's why aging and my body changing from having kids and eating too many chips and salsa didn't bother me much, because I knew he saw me—as an eighteen-year-old college freshman. We had lunch together for many weeks and even danced together at a club, but we always just "bumped into each other."

Finally, I got up the courage to ask him to a party I was hosting in my dorm room with my friend, Pam, from across the hall. I told him this would give me the chance to show him my photography portfolio. He said he would come to the party, and I was really, really excited about the possibility of our relationship turning into "a relationship," but the night of the party, the night I had waited for, he didn't show up at 7 PM as promised. I was so bummed he wasn't there, I went across the hall to my room to be alone and contemplate my love life. I was still technically dating my high school boyfriend, but I hardly talked to him and hadn't seen him in a couple months. I also was talking to a different guy, but I knew I was in love with Randy.

At 9:15 PM, there was a knock on my door, and it was Randy. He said, "Sorry I'm late, but I thought I should break up with my girlfriend before I came over here, and it took longer than I thought it would."

I was shocked by the news that he had a girlfriend. He was shocked that I really had a portfolio. But that was the official start of a relationship that would be amazing and envy-provoking.

For our first real, official date, Randy took me to the Smokehouse, a restaurant in downtown Lawrence, Kansas, that was famous for its BBQ. Before he picked me up, I was extremely nervous, trying to decide what to wear and how to do my hair. This nervousness was totally ridiculous; because of course he already knew what I looked like. We had been leading up to this date for eight months.

He thought the Smokehouse was so good, I guess, because it was one of the few places where college students used utensils when they ate. We either had dorm food or burgers, tacos, or pizza. I knew this meal was a financial sacrifice and certainly better than dorm food or the usual three burritos for ninety-nine cents I shared with my friend. Unfortunately, I just didn't like the smoke taste, but I ate it anyway. We talked and laughed and had fun.

I hadn't yet learned of his capacity to love or the level of his intelligence, which might have scared me away. I was totally smitten, though, because his eyes were the prettiest blue I had ever seen, and his body was beautiful. His smile was genuine, and he was always in a good mood.

After dinner, neither of us wanted the date to end, so we went next door for a beer. The drinking age back then was eighteen, if you were drinking 3.2% ABV beer. We sat at the bar, and he ordered two bowls of beer. The beer came in a dish the size of a serving bowl, thus the name, and I started to drink it. Even though I ate food I didn't like and drank beer I didn't like, I had never been more myself in my life than I was that night.

I learned two valuable lessons. One, to be authentic. Two... Well, the second lesson was a tough one. After about an hour in the bar, me having the best time of my life and trying really hard to drink the whole bowl of beer, I went to the bathroom and threw up both the BBQ and the beer.

Then, I didn't know what to do. I wanted to stay in the bathroom for fear I was going to throw up again, but finally, it was the last call. Randy started to bang on the door, asking if I was all right. He told me the bar was closing, that I had to come out. When I opened the door, I asked him to take me home right away. I was proud I didn't puke in his white 1975 Mercury Cougar.

When he pulled up in front of the dorm, he leaned over to kiss me goodnight, and I said, "Are you crazy? I'm not kissing you! I just threw up." I believe he thought I was playing hard to get, and that won him over. The night was incredible—but I still can't stand smoked meat or beer.

In May, the dorm I was living in had a formal dance, and I invited Randy. He wore a three-piece suit and an expensive tie, and it was the first time I had seen him in anything but a T-shirt and shorts. Over the years, I saw him in many suits, in many tuxes, in Hawaiian shirts, bathing suits, and his birthday suit. He wore an Air Force uniform for five years. But he always changed into a T-shirt and shorts as soon as possible. He hated dressing up and had absolutely no fashion sense. His favorite T-shirts supported causes and had some kind of logo on the back. The last time I saw him conscious, alive and well, happy and smiling, he was wearing a T-shirt and shorts, thirty-one years after the first time I saw him. Many people asked me over the years what the secret of a happy marriage was, and I always said: Randy Polk.

* * *

After Randy died, I looked at the over fifty T-shirts in his wardrobe and had no idea what to do with them. They were worn out, torn, and stained. I didn't want to give them away because I knew, if I did, I would end up seeing them on one of the many disadvantaged people I saw weekly, when we fed the homeless. I was worried about that freaking me out.

When he was alive, I frequently (and strongly) encouraged him to get rid of some of his old T-shirts, but now nothing seemed right. A few of them, I kept to wear when I needed to, but the rest were there just to look at. Then I heard about a T-shirt quilt, and I knew I would do that with the help of my talented friend, Laura. Randy had enough shirts to make two quilts, one for each son. I knew before I ever started that they would be flawed and sloppy, maybe even corny with the Superman backing I planned to use. I also knew our grown sons would wrap themselves in these quilts and remember and cry and laugh. They would feel grateful and cheated, simultaneously.

My weekend with Wesley was over. I didn't know how I was going to drive Bagel and myself back from College Station to Abilene, but I knew I had to do it. Justin had driven us there, but he had to stay in the area and take care of some business in Houston. I wouldn't be alone long. He and Wesley were going to meet me in Phoenix in a few days for Thanksgiving.

But with one exception, I had not driven more than a few miles from where I lived in twenty-five years. I just didn't drive on highways, overpasses, or long distances, which I know sounds ridiculous, but two things are relevant. One, I come from a long line of terrible drivers; I even flunked Driver's Ed. Two, when you are married for a long time, you take on roles, and you get comfortable. Randy liked to drive, so I let him. I cooked; he did yard work. In hindsight, letting him do all the driving was a mistake.

On September 8, 2001, I had flown to Phoenix to visit my new baby nephew, the first child born to my younger brother Geoff and his wife, Nanette. Randy and the kids stayed home; it was supposed to be a quick, three-day trip.

When I landed at the airport in Phoenix, my cell phone rang, and it was Randy wanting to know which pizza place I ordered from. By the end of the conversation, it was clear that it would be easier for me to order him and the boys a pizza from Arizona than to try to coach him through it. We had our roles, and one of mine was supplying the family with food. For years I teased him that he couldn't even order his own pizza, because he needed me so much.

On the morning of 9/11, my sister-in-law's screaming awakened me. I jumped out of bed and ran into the other room, assuming something horrible had happened to the baby.

Nanette was holding him, and he looked fine, but tears were rolling down her face. She pointed to the TV, where I saw the replay of the Twin Towers of the World Trade Center collapsing

I started crying and immediately called Randy, who was already glued to the TV, waiting for me to wake up. (In Arizona, we were three hours behind New York.) My family started calling to check on each other. We were all most concerned for our youngest sibling, Laurie, who lived a couple blocks from the Towers. We could not get through to New York, but eventually heard from Hawaii that she was safe, though still in New York. A couple hours before I was supposed to catch the plane back to Texas, I learned that all the flights had been grounded. My parents called to tell me to stay put, that I was safe, and I would get to come home eventually. Randy called to tell me to go rent a car quickly, before they were all gone. He knew me well and knew I would want to be with him and the kids. We waited all day, unable to believe what was happening, but when I realized the airport was not going to open up, I left for home.

I drove south to Tucson then stayed parallel to the border all the way to El Paso, feeling very safe, with all the Border Patrol already on high alert.

I spent the night in El Paso and the next day drove the rest of the 900 miles home, listening to horror stories on the radio for thirteen hours After that unplanned and traumatic road trip, I was so tired and anxious and glad to be home that I hadn't driven any long distances since. It wasn't planned; I just didn't do it.

About an hour from College Station, on the first of what would become many solo road trips, I called our close friend, Paul, who had lost his mother when he was a young college student—Wesley's age. How had he gotten through it? I wanted an instruction book on how to help my kids, even though I was still too unstable to do much.

Paul said he didn't grieve, he just went back to school, pretending nothing had happened. He regretted that now. In that one short conversation, he inadvertently gave me permission to feel what I needed to feel, grieve the way I wanted to grieve. Anyone who didn't like it would have to deal with it, and there were many in that camp. Maybe the way the Western world grieved, especially the Christian world, was not the most emotionally healthy way to do it. I thought from that moment on when someone asked me how I was, I didn't tell them, "Fine." I told them the truth.

I lost a lot of friends, but the ones who stuck around were the best people in the world. It is so hard to listen to and watch someone else's pain, and not everyone can do it. I knew this because, years earlier, a friend of mine lost her husband, and I would have done anything for her to make the pain go away. I knew I couldn't, of course, but my presence was a lifeline for her. Now that I needed a lifeline, I was extremely grateful for the ones who stepped up.

CHAPTER 6

ON THE THIRTIETH DAY after death, facing my first Thanksgiving without Randy, I was sitting at DFW airport, waiting for my flight to Phoenix and then the drive to Sedona. Randy was supposed to be here, and he wasn't, and I felt so alone.

I knew I could call someone, but I didn't feel like talking. The last time I was on an airplane with Randy we had one free upgrade to first class, because he had reached Million Miler status with American Airlines. It made me so mad that he was the one with the Million-Miler status, because I was the one who had done most of the shopping that had earned those miles on our VISA card. We fought over who would get the first-class seat, but I finally surrendered and gave it to him, because his hip hurt so much.

One of the many, many trials of dealing with death is trying to change all the accounts from joint to individual accounts. You need a lot of death certificates, because everyone wants one; evidently faking your spouse's death is a thing. American Airlines would not transfer Randy's Million-Miler status to me, and I was demoted in rank.

I was mad at the airport, I was angry with American, and I was furious at all the old people at the airport with me, because they were still alive and Randy wasn't. I hated all the couples, because they were couples, and my couple-hood had been stolen. Besides, I had no one to watch my luggage while I went to the bathroom. This rage against the injustice of it all was new to me. Up until then, I did not have anger issues. I was pretty laid back. Now I had it—but at least the anger was better than despair.

On Thanksgiving, everyone was kind and tried to act as normal. As the family was setting the table, we realized there wasn't any ice, and someone had to go buy a bag. No one volunteered. If Randy had been there, he would gladly have gone and bought ice. Before he left, we would need to reinforce for him what time dinner started because he was an explorer and had a way of losing track of time, but he would have gone on the errand gladly. I began to cry and went to my room. This was Day 33 of crying. I did not get off for a holiday.

The next day, I decided to take a walk. The weather and scenery in Sedona were beautiful, and I had the thought that feeling sorry for myself wasn't who I was. I no longer knew who I was, because I was no longer a wife, no longer a best friend, no longer a lover. I didn't yet know if I had lost my faith, but it did occur to me that if God didn't answer prayers, there wasn't much point in praying. Plus, all that victimhood was wearing on me, so I started a gratitude list in my head. On the top of the list, I was grateful to have been married to Randy Polk. That was as far as I got.

A couple of days earlier, when I was going through his desk, I found a gratitude list he had written eight months before he died.

1. Marla's great cooking
2. Putting on soft cotton socks when your feet are cold
3. Seeing artists at work
4. A musician hitting the right keys
5. A great conductor and orchestra
6. Singing or humming because you are happy
7. A mama bird feeding her babies
8. Koala bears and panda bears
9. A cat licking and cleaning her kittens
10. The determination of a turtle or inchworm or snail to get somewhere
11. A geyser
12. National forests
13. National monuments
14. The top of a mountain
15. Sailing
16. Floating in the water
17. Ziplining across valleys and waterfalls
18. Botanical gardens
19. A baby flipping a plastic spoon up and down in his mouth
20. Hot tubs and swimming pools
21. Caribbean, Mediterranean, and Greek Islands
22. The Dead Sea
23. Food made by the Druids
24. The Red Sea
25. The Sea of Galilee
26. Lox
27. Salads of Israel
28. Swiss Alps
29. Lake Geneva

30. Boat trip
31. Seeing our sons make significant decisions and following the Lord
32. Our friends and times together
33. Cookouts
34. Our fence that has a mural of flowers on it
35. Marla's singing
36. Marla's decoupage
37. God's downloads and visions for my art
38. My eye for scenery in picture form
39. Red River community center line dancing
40. 4th of July at Red River
41. Fireworks
42. Captaining my boat full of people
43. Taking kids wakeboarding
44. Taking kids skiing
45. Having kids in our "safe" house when they were growing up
46. Playing games like Love Your Neighbor with the family
47. Christmas
48. Good Friday at the Bowen ranch

* * *

I flew home from Sky Harbor alone, dreading my empty house, dreading the few days I would be alone before Wesley came back for a month. I landed in Abilene at our little airport and found my friends there to greet me and welcome me home. It was so kind. My friends hadn't left me—they were my lifelines. I began to realize they never would.

As I made my way around the house I had lived in and loved for twenty-five years, I began to hate it. I had so much stuff, and I no longer liked any of it. I was starting to hate all material possessions. It was so clear to me now that what really mattered were relationships; everything else was just in the way. I went to lunch with a friend and told her I would gladly trade everything I had, all my comforts, to live in a box under a bridge, if only I could live in it with Randy. And I meant it. In fact, I started fantasizing about being homeless and cold and sick and tired, so that my physical pain could match my emotional pain.

I was counting my life in days since Randy left us. At Day 44, I was still waking up and having to go through the realization all over again that he was dead. Then, I would start again through my list of what-ifs. What if I had checked on him sooner, instead of watching *Grey's Anatomy?*

What if he'd done another round of pre-op tests?

What if I'd left the phone in the bedroom? Our last kiss had been the breath I breathed into his mouth before beginning chest compressions. The next time I saw him, he had tubes sticking out of his mouth and everywhere else.

There was another development. Not only was I beginning to hate all my stuff, I was looking at all of Randy's stuff with confusion. *What do I do with it?* When he was alive, I was always asking him to clean out his office, to throw out some of the ridiculous junk he'd thought he had to keep: His textbooks and papers from college, for example.

One essay he wrote while getting his MBA did vindicate him and his packrat tendencies, though. The assignment was to think of an original idea for a product and then develop a marketing plan. His idea was to put vitamins in water, and he was very proud of his design. This was 1985, though, and he received a C- on the assignment, because his professor said that vitamins in water were a stupid idea and no one would buy it. Vitamin Water did not hit the market until 2000.

In a lot of ways, Randy was ahead of his time, and in a lot of ways, he was old-fashioned. His desk was littered with little scraps of paper filled with notes to himself. He had his baby clothes and toys from when he was a kid, every medal and ribbon earned becoming an Eagle Scout, plus collections of rocks and glass and barbed wire. He also had every card anyone had ever given him, every anniversary card, every birthday card and Father's Day card. The fact that he had kept them communicated how much these cards meant to him.

It was all junk, but the junk suddenly became priceless. Should I purge the stuff now that the only person in the world that could possibly ever want it was dead? What if somebody else wanted a *National Geographic* from 1972? Should I keep it knowing it could become a shrine? Every day, I found myself going into the office or the garage or the storage room to look at Randy's stuff and cry. I missed him terribly, but I found I also missed myself. I no longer recognized me.

When Randy and I started really getting to know each other, in the spring of 1983, he told me with great pride that he had read a novel once—that is one novel, one time. It was Robin Cooke's, *Coma*. He explained the plot of the book to me in great detail and how much he'd enjoyed it, how it completely took over his life. He didn't get anything else done until the book was finished, and that drove him crazy. Consequently, after that, he only read nonfiction: it wasn't all-consuming, and he could put it down if he had to.

When I asked my brilliant boyfriend if he had done the required reading for high school, books like *Pride and Prejudice* or *Of Mice and Men,* he vaguely remembered the titles but confessed he probably read the CliffsNotes. I assumed, wrongly, that he didn't have many books, but he had more books than most people. He loved books. When he got interested in a subject, he collected as many books on it as he could. (These were the days before Google.) He told me one of his musthaves, if he ever got to buy a house, was an office with a lot of bookshelves. He never went anywhere without something to read and usually bought more, any time we passed a bookstore.

I would tell him about the wonderful authors or great books I was reading. I tried reading him excerpts from my current story, but he wanted no part of that kind of commitment.

His sweet parents gave him a subscription to *Discover* and *National Geographic* every year, and he did read those. Even now, those magazines continued to be delivered with a cruel regularity that taunted me whenever I went to the mailbox. I counted 574 *National Geographic* magazines on bookshelves in his office. He couldn't ever bring himself to dispose of them, because he had them dated all the way back to 1963. They say that one man's treasure is another's trash, but the reverse is also true. I've asked the kids and Randy's family and friends if anyone wanted 574 *National Geographic* magazines, but no one did. Go figure.

In his beautifully constructed and beautifully messy office, Randy had eighteen Christian Bibles, twenty-two Jewish Bibles, two Korans, twenty-five books commenting on Bibles, seventy-five books on spiritual topics, twenty-two books about Israel, every textbook he'd ever bought for school—he didn't believe in selling his textbooks back, in case he needed them, twenty-two books on travel, five atlases, sixteen books about presidents, mostly focusing on President Polk, who was a great, great, great-uncle of his, twenty-eight on motivational subjects, such as how not to procrastinate, twelve on golf, thirty-eight on business, and also thirty-eight on health, which obviously didn't do him any good. There were thirteen on magic, sixteen on gambling, eight on art, and twenty-six on computers. Twelve old and maybe rare books on various subjects, fifteen beautiful coffee table books, and twenty-two books of ghost stories. Ah, and I'm forgetting the set of encyclopedias and a full set of "how-to" books covering everything from A to Z. But there wasn't one novel. If Randy were here and you asked him how many of these books he'd read, he would flash a smile that would turn into a mischievous half-smile, and he would raise his eyebrows, and say, "Not many, but I have them if I want to read them."

In 1999, our friend Pam sent Randy a novel for their shared birthday. It was about a woman who went on a walkabout with aborigines, and she sent it because it was a great adventure story, and Randy was everyone's ultimate carrier of the adventure flag. She knew he would want to read it and then go on a walkabout himself. The gift caused Randy great angst, because he didn't read novels, but he finally agreed to read it because he couldn't let Pam down. If he did something, he was all in. Though it was not a very long book, he cleared his calendar anyway and read it for many hours straight, until it was finished. I just reread this book, *Mutant Message Down Under*, and felt as if it were written just for me, to instruct me on how to let go of Randy's stuff but never Randy. It is incredible how these connections work, and the thought is never far from my mind, wondering whether, somehow, Randy might be orchestrating them.

When the Internet became commonplace, Randy would spend hours and hours researching subjects. If he came across an article that he thought one of his family members or good friends would want, he would print it and give it to them to read. He absolutely valued knowledge and the pursuit of knowledge. If he came across a website that he might want to visit in the future, like how to carve a pumpkin, he would print it and file the copy. He had many old magazine and newspaper articles saved and archived on every subject, from how to have a successful marriage (which he obviously did read) to counting cards in Vegas.

When he wanted to give the boys a concrete understanding of the famous irrational number, pi, he told his computer to "print pi," and it printed for hours. 3.14159265358979328346... It went on for hundreds of pages. He showed the pages to the boys and it was hilarious—and no one laughed at the joke harder than he did. My first college degree was in environmental science, so I was happy that he did recycle the pi paper.

When Justin became a competitive chess player at eight years old, Randy researched chess for him and enrolled him in online courses. And he bought him every book on chess ever written, which Justin never read, but he had them just in case he wanted to.

Once, a close friend's nephew was killed in a car accident, and her son, who was working on a crew traveling with a rock band, couldn't be reached. Randy located the band's tour schedule online, noted the band members' names, got their hometowns from their bios, and tracked down their relatives

Eventually, someone got word to the son to call home. Randy would have made a great detective, though he never read mysteries.

In 2001, Randy's dad, Travis, was diagnosed with terminal cancer. Randy spent countless hours on the computer learning about his disease, and this knowledge eventually helped his father get into an experimental trial, because Randy tracked down the research doctor's private number and called him. It was indeed a miracle that his dad survived. None of us will understand why he received that miracle and, twelve years later, his son did not, so Travis had to watch him die.

CHAPTER 7

RANDY AND I HAD the privilege to travel a lot—and the duty. Our families were scattered across many different states, so we were always flying somewhere to visit them. We also did a lot of traveling taking Justin to chess tournaments. When Justin was five, he started playing chess, and by the time he was eight, he had won third in the United States Open and first in Texas in elementary school. Randy loved to travel with him all over the country to watch him play. Wesley and I tagged along, usually finding something else to do. Randy had fun doing everything including watching chess.

Sometimes we traveled just to fulfill Randy's ongoing mission to have fun. We both loved seeing new places, but the plane rides to reach them were very predictable. I would get the window seat, and he would take the aisle. He always brought a carry-on, and in it were the latest *National Geographic* and *Discover* magazines, a puzzle book on Sudoku, pencils, gum, a protein bar, his Garmin GPS, his camera, and a phone charger. He rarely got around to reading his magazines, because he always bought a newspaper at the airport and was prone to become fascinated with some articles in the magazine in the seat pocket in front of him.

Randy didn't like to watch television, unless it was the news or a ball game. He never watched sitcoms or dramas. He never allowed the kids to have TVs in their rooms, for fear they might waste time. It's ironic how many hours of television I now watch just to survive. Randy eventually started watching reality shows and loved *Survivor* and *Naked and Afraid*. If he had been younger when those shows came out, I have no doubt he would have applied to be on them. Most weekend nights, because we had a room full of kids over, he watched what they wanted to watch. He sat in his recliner and laughed and fully earned his reputation as the coolest and most fun dad around.

The kids talked freely around him, and though he always supported them one hundred percent and never judged them, he was very clear on the importance of good choices. The kids always knew ours was a safe house with a zero-tolerance policy for drugs or alcohol (for the kids). He even confronted a few of them when they were making some bad choices, always telling them he loved them, no matter what. He himself never took an illegal drug because he was afraid he might like them too much, so he never risked starting.

I also loved the kids, but did not show it by staying up late with them. I showed my love by cooking and by listening to their teenage dramas. I did not buy into their dramas but did listen actively and told them they could do better. Somehow, we made a great team, because the kids loved hanging out with us. I am still a friend to many of these young adults today.

* * *

On my own, I didn't know how to start going through the fifty-three-years' worth of Randy's stuff, so instead, I went to Kansas. It was our first Christmas apart. My kids were worried that, without Randy, I wouldn't want to continue my relationship with his family, the kids' grandparents, cousins, aunts, and uncles, but this was the furthest thing from the truth. Randy's family were the ones who loved him the most, and I wanted to be around them and talk about him.

I soon found out that grieving is a very individual thing, however. I was grieving and didn't care who knew it, but they were not in the same place. They were thankful. I was angry. They talked about how blessed they felt, having had Randy for as long as they did. I said we had been cheated out of thirty or more years with him and maybe more, if he had lived to be a hundred, like he thought he would.

They wanted to carry on with comforting holiday traditions, and I now hated the traditions, because Randy wasn't participating in them. His mom, Carolynn, said what a joy it was to be a grandparent and how much she loved her grandchildren. Of course, I started to cry, thinking about Randy never becoming a grandparent. He would have made a wonderful grandfather. It was then that I started thinking about trying to write stories about Randy, to share with his grandkids, so they could somehow get to know him. It is hard to grieve with others, but it is worse grieving alone. That first Christmas was a blur to me. I remember spending a lot of time in my in-laws' guest bedroom, crying at the unfamiliarity of all the familiar people and traditions. There was much debate about whether hanging Randy's stocking was a good idea. They ultimately did, but Santa did not fill it.

I never thought I would look at the calendar with the filter of before and after death, but this is my reality. Even though it was the hardest place to be, with my precious in-laws on Christmas, without Randy, I can't imagine being anywhere else. As I walked around their house, Randy is everywhere and nowhere simultaneously. It was the pictures on the walls. It was his spirit. It was sitting around the table, not seeing him in his usual spot. It was wondering for a millisecond what mischief he was getting into, about which child he was challenging to the latest video game, before remembering he wasn't coming back.

Looking at the card table, I remembered the clicking of the Dominoes and Randy playing for hours with his dad and his uncle, drinking a beer and watching football while complaining about the bones they'd picked. Randy could have given seminars on the art of relaxing and enjoying his family, but that would have been counterproductive. When we played games like Catch Phrase or Scattergories, he would laugh so hard—usually at himself—that his feet would actually lift up off the ground, while he doubled over and stomped the air. His eyes would disappear, and he would wipe tears of joy from their corners with his big fists.

He got really excited about the food for Christmas dinner and always took more than he could eat, because he loved the idea of a Christmas feast. In the twenty-eight Christmases I got to spend with him, I never saw him cook anything, volunteer to clean up anything, shop for presents, or prepare in any way. The hustle and bustle of Christmas didn't faze him. He was totally content and shameless in his role as a good-time maker and joy giver. He never even decorated the Christmas tree—he'd just pull it out of the garage and hand it over. Oh, he would make sure the lights worked and Christmas music was playing then just sat back and let others do the work.

He was the hardest-working man I knew at playing. It was a fantastic gift and an incredible legacy that he passed down to our children. Many times, I joked with him that he married me, a Jewish girl, so he didn't have to miss Christmas with his own family every other year. Of course, he trained me well to jump on the holiday bandwagon. Christmas was fun for me, and I loved decorating and wrapping presents and seeing my kids' eyes light up on Christmas morning. Hanukah was also exceptional, and we did a great job of celebrating, too. Still, it was not as exciting and did not have the rich heritage Christmas had for us. Maybe it was because we celebrated many Jewish holidays each year but we only celebrated Christmas and Easter, so we went all-out.

I see Randy in Justin's and Wesley's broad shoulders and in their bottomless blue eyes. I see him when my children look at me with so much more love than I deserve, because I remember how Randy also loved me more than I could comprehend. Without him, I didn't want to open presents or carry on as if nothing had changed, but I didn't want to steal those traditions from my children. They are a connection to their father, more tangible than most. So, I knew I would continue to be with the Polks at Christmastime.

I appreciate love that is real and which, consequently, has made my loss so much more real. I couldn't wait for the day when I wouldn't expect Randy to be there in the flesh, but I also dreaded that day. I longed for less pain, but I held onto it as I would hold onto Randy.

At least Randy got to spend every Christmas of his life with his family and he never had to experience the kind of heartbreaking loss that all of us now feel. He was lucky.

CHAPTER 8

I ONLY NEEDED TO RESCUE eight more animals to reach my announced target of ten, and I started to think about getting a Labradoodle.

Everyone warned me I would never find this cuddly and very in-demand breed in a shelter. Still, I didn't believe in buying pets when there was so many that needed rescuing.

On Christmas Eve, I called Wesley's girlfriend Maddie's mom, who rescued and fostered animals in the Dallas area, to ask her if she could find me a rescue doodle. I told her it had to be female, already house trained, and preferably blonde, so her fur would blend in with the floors in my house. All of these conditions diminished my chances significantly, but remarkably she found one for me on Christmas Day. The nine-month-old trained, female, blonde Labradoodle's owner had died, and now it was in foster care. The shelter called me for a telephone interview and, after a background check, said I could pick her up in a few days.

I knew this high-energy, still-a-puppy, part-lab would be good for me. Bagel, my constant companion, was very content to do nothing 24/7—kind of like me. This new dog would insist on my playing with her and walking her, and as intimidating as the thought of a new dependent was, I knew the added energy into my house was what I needed.

She arrived on December 30, and we started to get to know each other in the back yard. She immediately ran across the pool as if she thought the water was dry land, or maybe she had a Messiah complex. The cold water shocked her, and she started to sink, but she doggy paddled her way into my heart. Though I should have named her Peter, I stuck with the carbohydrate theme for naming pets and called her Farfalle.

Day 67 was New Year's Eve. Wesley wanted to go to a party at his friend's ranch, and I suggested to Justin that he go with him, that nobody needed to stay home with me. They both rejected the idea: if I didn't go, they weren't going. Since the party was for all ages, I agreed to go, so they wouldn't be deprived of the chance for a good New Year's Eve.

This was the first time since Randy died that I was with people I didn't know, and it was torture. All these kind people wanted to talk and enjoy themselves, and I found myself unable to make small talk, unable to do anything but think about getting out of there. What was I going to do at midnight? Who would I kiss? Like a caged animal, I considered my alternatives. I couldn't leave, because we were all in one car. Eventually, I found a safe place to hide, and I ushered in the New Year alone, which seemed very appropriate.

Randy and I had never been into big New Year's celebrations. We didn't like to mess with the crowds, pay for overpriced food and drinks, and watch for drunk drivers. Most of the time, we stayed home with friends and family, or even by ourselves: we were content to be alone together. The exception was 1995, when Randy and I decided to go to New York City and watch the ball drop.

We farmed the kids out to their grandparents and went to Times Square to spend a few days. We stayed at the Marriott Marquis on an upper floor, to give us a great view of Dick Clark from above. Randy had never been to New York, so, on the afternoon of December 31, we started to walk, trying to see everything we could see of Manhattan. The bitter cold was tolerable on that sunny day, and we didn't head back to the hotel until about 8 PM.

When we turned on Broadway, we found we could not get within a half mile of the Marriott. The police barricades were already up, and it seemed as if the expected one million people were already there. I do not have claustrophobia, nor am I typically crowd-phobic, but this vast, tightly packed throng was extreme; I was very uncomfortable and I was freezing. I could hardly turn around, there were so many people, most of them already working on their New Year's Eve buzz. I didn't want to spend hours on the street with the mob, and I was afraid I would lose Randy in the crowd; Randy, of course, loved it.

I asked several cops to let us past the barricade, so we could get to our hotel, but I had no luck. Randy could see my increasing anxiety and, begrudgingly, told me he would get us past the barricade. He went up to a different cop, smiled his smile, and before I knew it, we were on the safe side of the ropes with the VIP and the paparazzi. That wasn't enough for me. I continued to urge us toward the hotel, and finally we were through the doors and in the lobby. I ran to the elevator, anxious to get to our room and away from the mob. Once upstairs, I was very content to look out the window and see the festivities through the safety of glass and distance, but Randy looked like he'd lost his best friend and dropped his ice cream cone. He wanted to be in the fray, not on the sidelines.

"I've got to go back," he told me, and I nodded.

"Have fun and be careful."

So the new VIP elevatored back down to Times Square to enjoy all the perks associated with being on the right side of the barricade. He had the time of his life, alone and happy among the million who were there, while I enjoyed myself in the warmth and security of our room, content to watch out the window.

* * *

A whole new level of sadness engulfed me. It had been so bad before, I could not have imagined it getting worse, but it did. Every day, I had been telling myself I just had to do only one thing. Sometimes it was no more than taking a shower or paying a bill—nothing extraordinary for the old me. But on Day 78, I had no desire to do even that one thing. I didn't get out of bed except to pee and to walk the dogs. I cried because I missed Randy and missed being happy and having joy and making plans.

I missed Randy, and I missed me.

The crying lasted into Day 79. The first time I went to the grocery store after Randy's death was excruciating. It took me by surprise. I went to the same-old store, started along the same-old route, and realized that the stuff I was putting in the basket was all the foods Randy liked. Right there, next to the eleven different kinds of apples, I started sobbing.

After that breakdown, I no longer dreaded going out and making a fool out of myself. I mean, it couldn't get much worse. I might bump into people who would tell me they were so sorry, they had meant to call me, and told me that if I needed anything, I should just call them. As if I could call them. What would I say—"Hi, my life has fallen apart and my heart is broken. Can you fix that?" The ones who really wanted to help called me.

It scared me, this anger I had that kept bubbling out of me. I was angry that my heart had been broken and my joy stolen. A friend said, "Press into God, and He will comfort you," but there were many levels on which, He didn't comfort me. Most of my close friends were married. I was lonely, but I didn't want to be with people I was not close to. My married friends framed their world as a couple, and I got that. I used to be guilty of that. I was left continually asking, Now what?

On Day 80, I had hired a yoga instructor to come to my house for no better reason than because Pam told me to. Every night, she called to ask me questions, and I answered them before I cried, so it was progress. She was trying to assess my mental state long distance: Was I sad or was I clinically depressed? Maybe I was just circumstantially depressed, but most of my family members were suggesting antidepressants. They couldn't stand to see me like this, I thought; that is why they wanted to medicate me, not because it was in my best interest. I had nothing against pharmaceuticals, but, deep in my core, in a place I couldn't readily access, I knew, if I masked this pain, I would not come out the other side. If I numbed the pain, I would be numbing any chance of future joy. I did not know how I knew this, but for me, I knew I had to say no to Prozac.

A few friends had joined me in my first-ever yoga class. It was hard and distracting. I knew it was good for me, but I cried the whole time I downward-dogged and pigeoned and attempted various other grueling poses. After that first class was over, we were all drinking coffee when one of the ladies said, "That was so fun. We should try couple's yoga."

Day 81 started so horribly because I missed him so much the night before. The pain was so intense and awful, and I was so tired of it. I tried to do one thing to distract myself, and then I hated that, so I tried another. I had learned the definition of not being comfortable in my own skin.

Day 82: I woke from my recurring nightmare to the realization that Randy was still dead. I felt tired and hopeless. After just four hours of sleep or so, I had another Saturday, the worst day of the week.

I didn't have work to distract me. It was a family day for the rest of the world; once it was our day, but no longer. As much pain and loneliness as I felt during the rest of the week, it was nothing compared to Saturdays.

I turned on the TV, my constant companion, and I watched another episode of *Monk*. I identified with Monk missing his dead wife, Trudy. Her loss had sent him over the edge; I was holding on by a string.

I decided to try reading the Psalms. If there was no hope of relief for me in this world, maybe I could find it in the other world. At first, I couldn't see the words through my tears:

Answer me when I call to you, O my righteous God. Give me relief from my distress; be merciful to me and hear my prayer.

Day 83 was the day I decided to go to church again, thinking it would comfort me. As I was getting ready, I looked at Randy's toothbrush still in the holder. I left it there. I put on earrings; that was huge. I had quit wearing makeup and jewelry or caring about my appearance, but now I applied concealer to the bags under my eyes and put on lipstick. I did not put on eye makeup because of the tears I knew I couldn't control, but it was a milestone.

I went to the church Randy and I attended for twenty years, the church where his funeral service was held. I sat next to my ninety-year-old friend and resented her for her age. She hugged me, and I cried. And cried. She told me the way out of the pit was one rung at a time through praise. I couldn't think of anything to praise Him for, though.

I watched all the couples holding hands and putting their arms around each other, and I cried some more. As people came by to ask me how I was doing, they often mentioned someone they knew who was suffering, perhaps in an effort to make me feel better. It didn't. I thought that if going to church made me cry, maybe I should no longer go.

That night, I saw a beautiful sunset, and as I was watching it, "Wildfire" came on the radio. Randy was famous for his sunset images, and, in New Mexico, we had loved hearing Michael Martin Murphy on more than one occasion. It was a message from heaven. I was indeed comforted, and I smiled.

CHAPTER 9

Even after all this time, I was still filling my days with the business of death. I had to go to court for probate, so my friend, also my lawyer, Mike, went with me and talked about how much he loved Randy and about how his own father had died too young. I was glad for his conversation.

As I walked toward the bathroom, I passed the judge in the hallway. I did not know what my face looked like, but it must have worn its familiar look of despair.

The judge, not knowing me or what I was doing there, said, "Hello. And smile—it can't be that bad."

I went into the bathroom and cried. Moments later, when I appeared before him at the bench, he realized his mistake and said he was sorry, but I was wondering how a probate judge could be so insensitive.

Mike took me home, and I continued my daily routine. First, Randy's work, trying to keep the property management business running. Second, deal with my own continuing obligations. Third, either walk or do yoga and eat, so I could report to Pam that night that I was trying. I ended the day by tackling just one task associated with Randy. Was it time to get rid of his clothes? His toiletries? His eyeglasses? That day, I threw out the sunflower-seed shells in the bowl on his desk.

I stared at all his keys for an hour. He had a lot of them, because of the rental properties; now it fell to me deal with them, which was an honor and a curse. It seemed that he had multiples of every key, and even when the locks were changed, he never threw one away. In his car, in his pants, on the table, in the dresser, on a shelf, I found keys, few of them labeled. When I needed a key, in the course of trying to function without him, I usually had the lock rekeyed rather than try one after another until I found the right one; that seemed a form of self-torture. So Randy's keys were of no practical use to me, but still I did not know what to do with all of them. I did not want to become a hoarder—the prospect panicked me—but I couldn't bring myself to throw something out he touched. Once it was gone, it was gone forever, just like him.

I knew women who had bought and been given jewelry made out of keys by the homeless, through the nonprofit the Giving Key. I finally decided this was a solution I could live with. I took a picture of all seventy keys before I packed them up, a compromise that would allow me to purge Randy's stuff. I kept asking myself, why so many keys? (Why? was fast becoming my new mantra.) Keys represented doors being open, but Randy had the ability to open the door to almost everywhere, not because of his connections or influence, but because of his huge smile and his kind heart and very blue eyes. It was tough to say no to Randy.

So, again, why so many keys? He didn't need them. If he knocked, the door would be opened to him. He spent a lot of time outside, and he didn't need a key for that. The only explanation I have come up with for his obsession with keys, some from many locks ago, was that he was literally and figuratively a treasure hunter. When I met him, he used a metal detector, a hobby he started as a boy. When we went to the beach or an old homestead, he would hunt with his metal detector for hours while I sat and read a book, looking up smiling in delight when he found something lost.

Figuratively, Randy's keys represented the treasure chest he was continually unlocking in me and our kids, and he always seemed to have the right key. He certainly had the key to my heart, as well as the key to the kingdom, and the key to puzzles of all kinds, which he loved doing. (His latest obsession was *Words with Friends*.) In his own low-key way, he loved being the center of attention. He had a great singing voice, and always sang on key; he could play the piano by ear and was an accomplished trumpet player.

In my grief, I decided he could not part with his keys because they represented the key to life, and he lived every second as if it were vital. You would think, with so many keys, he might be afraid of losing some, but I was the one who was always losing things—my keys, my phone, or, if I was driving, my sense of direction. Randy, by contrast, had a great sense of direction and always helped me locate my lost stuff.

Usually he started by dumpster-diving on the assumption I had inadvertently thrown out the missing item with the trash. (I used to really like to throw things away.) Ironically, he found me and now I was lost without him.

As I packed up the keys to mail, so the homeless could have jobs, I also thought about Randy's relationship with the homeless community in our town. For six years, we had fixed dinner for the hungry and/or homeless in our community. At first, he barbequed in the front yard of the Palm House for the people in that vulnerable neighborhood, which really seemed to help strengthen the area--probably because Randy was really friendly, didn't know a stranger, and made everyone feel as if they were worth talking to.

Eventually, we had so many people coming to eat, we had to move locations to a bigger facility, and so we partnered with a soup kitchen. We fed them on Sunday nights, Randy and me and teams of other volunteers all cooking and hanging out with "our neighbors."

The day after his funeral, my sons and their friends went to the Sunday night dinner. They served in place of Randy and me, not wanting to disappoint the 100 people who looked forward to the meals and fellowship and counted on them.

When they returned from volunteering that night, Wesley told me a story I had not heard before. Wesley, like his father, was an explorer. He and his friends loved to find abandoned buildings or remote trails in our small city and look around for treasures. It gave them the adrenaline rush of the unknown without getting into too much trouble. One day, they found a trail very close to some abandoned buildings downtown, left their car, and walked about a mile. What made that trail so interesting was its remoteness in the middle of the city.

Eventually, they came to a vast homeless encampment, where a very mean, ugly dog started growling to protect its territory. The teenagers froze, not knowing what to do, when, suddenly, Randy appeared with a man, who called off the dog. They were relieved to see Randy, and he was quite shocked to see them. Randy, it turned out, had been coming to the homeless encampment about once a week since stumbling across it a year earlier, to bring food and hang out with the friends he made.

In time, I went back to the Sunday night meal because I missed my neighbors, but doing something positive and doing it without Randy was harder than I'd anticipated. I was not much help that first night back night; I sat in the back and cried. I kept going back, though, and each week I spent less and less time by myself and more time with the people. It really did help me to have somewhere to go and to realize I was not the only one in the world with pain and genuine problems.

I met a homeless man named Randy, and the name gave us an immediate connection. I asked him about his life and, respectfully, asked him about how he became homeless. He told me that, ten years earlier, his wife, the love of his love, had died suddenly in a car accident. He said, after that, he started drinking and eventually got addicted to meth, because he couldn't face life without her.

I totally empathized, and his story taught me a valuable lesson: If I didn't try harder to move forward, my life could and would get a lot worse.

CHAPTER 10

IT WAS DAY 84, and I realized my life was now in slow motion. I moved slower, and time moved tortoise-like. I continued to process the pain slowly, knowing if it came at me all at once, I would not survive.

I was not happy or comfortable anywhere. Home was sad and lonely. I would get in the car to drive but couldn't figure out where I wanted to go. More often than not, I ended up in my now too familiar go-to, Randy's office chair. If I could do anything creative, I thought, maybe I could release some dopamine, and that would make me feel better. Scattered on Randy's desk were all the scraps of paper with notes in his handwriting, magazine articles he had cut out, lyrics to a song he had printed. It occurred to me I could decoupage this snapshot of his beautiful, distracted mind and I glued all of the papers to wooden magazine racks for my kids.

The act of the cutting and pasting was so simple –and surprisingly uplifting. The dopamine was working. Better still, without throwing anything out, I had cleared away a lot of debris from Randy's office, and I had gifts for my kids, something new from their dad. And this didn't have to be the end of it: I could continue to provide them with mementos from his life, on occasions when they would especially miss him—Father's Day, his birthday. They could look forward to repeated surprises from their dad.

One of the many hardest parts of losing Randy was the loss of human contact. Because my sadness was so overwhelming, the thought of intimacy did not cross my mind, but my need for touch was great and not easy to replace. I petted my animals and thought about finding a baby to rock. In the midst of these poor substitutes, Angie, Randy's massage therapist, was another lifeline. She came to my house once a week, knowing I wasn't ready to get out regularly, and brought her table, so she could give me a massage in my bedroom. Usually, throughout the whole hour, I would cry, and she would listen to my tears and rub away the tension.

On day 85, I did get dressed (not a given) and faced the reality that my computer had crashed and the plumbing had backed up. Actually, I didn't really face it. I just cried and cried, feeling a new level of anxiety and anger, because Randy wasn't there to take care of these things. I wanted to die, because I wasn't up to the challenge of wastewater all over the floor and dealing with a computer on the fritz. Living was what was scary, not dying. Despite this breakdown, I kept an appointment I had to tour an apartment building Randy had been working on when he died. Keeping the appointment wasn't a show of strength, it was simply less demanding than rescheduling.

The building was leased below value to New Beginnings, a nonprofit, to be used as a transitional home for women needing a new start in life. Randy had been proud to make this happen.

The apartments looked great. Could Randy see how great they looked? I hoped so.

There was an older man there, a widower, who told me the grieving would never stop, but I would have joy in the midst of the grieving. Boy, did that piss me off! However true it might have been, I was not ready to hear it. At the end of yet another incredibly horrible day, I decided to have company for dinner for the first time since Randy died—just a couple of my lifelines, and we ordered in. Still, it was a milestone. In my previous life, I had loved to entertain and did it often. On this occasion, I set the table for six instead of five out of habit, forgetting Randy wasn't with us. I silently watched as my friend took the plate away. Despite, the newest realization that Randy was gone, the evening turned out all right.

We started talking about our yoga class, and Geoff, my brother from another mother, did a warrior pose to prove he could do yoga. In the process, he knocked a whole pitcher of tea off the counter, and we started laughing. I laughed so hard my gut hurt, and it felt good. Maybe the old widower was right when he tried to explain simultaneous grief and joy.

* * *

In the year 2000, when one of my best friend's husband died of cancer, I took it very hard. I was Latimer's lifeline, and it was excruciating to watch her grief and pain and the grief and pain of her children. At the time of her loss, she was forty-nine years old, the same age I was when I lost Randy. Many people assumed she would be a great comfort to me, but that first couple of months, she wasn't. Thirteen years after her loss, she was okay and thriving. I wanted to gain inspiration from her, but I had watched her travel the road I was on, and I couldn't face it. Right after her beloved husband died, she woke up every day and said, "Today I want to be a blessing to someone."

I didn't wake up with that kind of inspiration, but it was true that some days were better than others. On one of them, I received a phone call from a young man who worked at the Palm House, the outreach house I had been overseeing for several years. Was there room in the budget to buy some tools to leave at the Palm House? Inspiration struck. Randy had a whole garage full of tools he certainly wasn't ever going to need again. I was able to transfer some of Randy's tools to the Palm House, a gift that was especially appropriate, since he had been the volunteer maintenance man for the place. Of course, I couldn't help but think that Randy himself should be the one giving the tools away. He had about three or more versions of every tool, because he never could find the right one and went and bought another one for each job, and would have gladly given a set of tools to the Palm House. Randy was very generous.

Many years ago, he had been more attached to his things—maybe because we had less stuff in those days. As he grew older (but not old enough), he learned that stuff was just stuff. Randy came to understand that when he lent a tool to someone, a neighbor or stranger, he shouldn't expect to get it back. There was no reason for hard feelings. He learned this lesson slowly, but once he got it, he got it. I may have contributed to this lesson.

I was always loaning Randy's stuff without his permission, so he had to learn to hold on loosely. For example, in 1996, I let the babysitter use our car when we went to Kansas to visit family. I received a call from her while Randy was tossing a ball up and down. The babysitter had been in an accident; she was okay, but the car was not. Since I had "forgotten" to tell Randy that I'd loaned the car in the first place, now I had to tell him about that and the accident at the same time. The cadence of his ball-throwing never changed; I might as well have told him about the weather. It was just a car; he didn't care.

Randy was generous in so many ways, and the more generous he became, the more financially able he was to be generous. He loved going out to eat, and he always paid for anyone who allowed him to. At Christmas, he always gave money to our kids to give to the bell ringers for the Salvation Army; a small thing, but he wanted them to see generosity in action.

Once in a while, he knew he was supposed to do something special for someone. For instance, he loved hosting entertaining, over-the-top parties for our employees. One year, he told them to all come back to work for a critical meeting. There was no critical meeting; instead, a limo arrived to take everyone to a gourmet dinner in another town.

The gifts were not always extravagant or expensive, but he gave them with absolutely no strings attached.

Randy also liked getting gifts for himself, and he firmly believed he was worth it. On June 20, 1994, the day our second son was born, our ancient refrigerator completely failed, so the day we came home from the hospital, Randy had to go to the mall to buy a new one. I was not in any shape to shop after my C-section, so he went by himself. Many hours later, he returned to his new baby and recuperating wife, with two new jet skis, but no refrigerator!

On the way to Sears, he had walked through a watercraft show in the middle of the mall. By the time he had made his irresistible purchases, Sears was closing, so we had to do without a fridge. On the bright side, my eighty-four-year-old grandfather and seventy-seven-year-old grandmother, who were visiting to help with baby Wesley and three-year-old big brother Justin, got to go on their first jet-ski ride. It was a delight to watch them, although I myself, fresh out of surgery, didn't get to try the jet-skis until the next season. I had every reason to be mad—not only did we have to wait for a fridge, but also, Randy had made a considerable purchase without my knowledge or agreement. Believe me, I shared those thoughts—just home from giving birth I was not at my hormonal best—but I made the decision that day to embrace Randy's adventuresome spirit and to choose peace instead of conflict. It really wasn't a sacrifice, and Randy's adventurous spirit rarely let me down. A few years later, he sold the jet skis to his sister for a dollar.

Randy never thought it an imposition when he took Justin and Wesley and several friends to water parks or on lake trips. He regularly paid for everything, because it didn't feel right to him to get money from kids, friends, family, or the less fortunate. Unexpectedly, he was also able to receive gifts and did so with gusto.

In one of his generous moods, Randy gave some dear friends two all-expense-paid trips to Israel. He wanted them to experience what was in his opinion the most spiritual and safe place on Earth. We ourselves went to Israel three times, and if he had lived, I'm sure we would have gone many more. Both our sons were bar mitzvahed in Szfat, Israel, in our own private service for our own unique religion. We had the honor of using an ancient Torah, all arranged by our spiritual guide and friend Sam Peak.

That first trip to Israel was fascinating and very peaceful, though it did at times get tedious for a ten- and thirteen-year-old. When I saw they needed a break from the historical lectures, I would give them money, cards, and poker chips to keep them busy.

Justin was fascinated with poker, and his goal was to learn to count cards and, when he was twenty-one, go to Vegas to become a professional poker player. Naturally, Randy thought this was a worthy goal and wanted to go with him. Competitive poker turned out to be harder than he expected, though, and by the time he turned twenty-one, he was on his way to becoming a professional engineer.

Randy was invited to play poker about once a month, a friendly game with low stakes, but poker is poker, and some of the guys were very competitive. The first time Randy showed up, he brought a briefcase filled with money, and he wore dark glasses and a huge gold chain. The other guys could not help but laugh. In one moment, Randy had reminded them to have fun and enjoy each other's company.

His generosity went beyond financial. When Bryce, a seventeen-year-old friend of Wesley's needed a place to stay, Randy insisted we open our home to him. Bryce was not getting along with his parents, and we worried, if we didn't take him in, he would drop out of school and make some really poor choices. We let him stay with us because we believed it was the right thing to do, and we had the pleasure and emotional hardship of having this young man live with us for five months. Randy wanted nothing other than Bryce's wellbeing and peace, and he lived to see that happen in a big way.

In one area, Randy was not generous at all: he was downright selfish about his time. Once, years ago, he was asked to be on a committee. He lasted one meeting; the discussion was boring to him and even a little unpleasant, so he quit. He never served on another board or committee afterward, and that was in 1992.

Maybe he always knew he would run out of time. He never planned on doing things someday. If they were worth doing, he wanted to do them ASAP. Everything else came in second to what he really enjoyed doing. He never went to funerals or weddings because it was expected, but only when he wanted to. Randy taught me a great lesson when it came to saying yes and saying no. I would frequently accuse him teasingly of being a selfish son of a bitch when he said no regularly.

I now know that because of his ability to say no to others, he gave his family more time than most husbands and fathers who live twice as long. He really liked spending his time with our kids and me. He always had enough time for us and very rarely told us no. My husband definitely took generosity and selfishness to a new level. I always had a nagging feeling that he would die too soon. Even so, I never saw it coming.

CHAPTER 11

AT THE END OF JANUARY, 2014, over Days 90-94 A.D., I thought it would be a good idea to invite my four close friends—Pam, Latimer, Mandy, and Candy—to stay at my parents' house in Sedona, Arizona. My parents were going out of town, so we had the house to ourselves, and I thought the trip would do me good.

I still had not recovered my social etiquette, but I was trying hard to act normal, so we went for a pedicure, a typical girls' outing. The nail lady told me I had waited too long, that I should have a pedicure once a month. I told her I hadn't had a pedicure in three months because my husband had died and I'd died, too, and didn't care what my toes looked like. She was quiet after that.

Most of those days in Sedona are a blur to me. Trauma does strange and horrible things to your brain. I remember hiking a little, and we went on a Jeep ride with a weird guide. Mostly, what I remember is my friends talking a lot about their husbands.

It was Super Bowl weekend, and I could not wrap my head around the fact that the teams would be playing without Randy there to watch them. I didn't sleep much the night before, so, though I got up Sunday morning, I didn't stay up long. I lay in bed and wailed, while my four friends took turns trying to comfort me. Latimer quoted Jeremiah 29:11, "'For I know the plans I have for you,' declares the Lord, 'plans to prosper you and not to harm you, plans to give you hope and a future."

The scripture failed to comfort me. Instead, it really messed with my head. I screamed, *"How did this apply to Randy?"*

Finally, I fell back to sleep, thinking, *will this pain never stop?* It was unbearable, even with love and breathtaking scenery surrounding me. Even that was still not enough. It was like I had been dropped off in a foreign country, without knowing the language or having a map.

Randy and I had been traveling to Sedona since my parents moved there in 1994. We made many trips there with the family, gathering with all my siblings and stepsiblings. There was fun and laughter and always a family photo. In 2000, we invited Pam and Vince and their boys to vacation with us there. The boys were all under ten at the time, so the most exciting adventures involved only Randy and Vince. They would go out while Pam and I enjoyed staying home with the kids.

If I had to describe Randy with one word, it would be an adventurer. He decided where he was going based on whether or not he had been there before. If he was driving down the road and passed a route he hadn't driven down, he took it. This worked well on leisurely trips with no agenda. It didn't work well when he was in sales, where his territory covered several counties and he had to make a quota. Early on, I learned to appreciate his sense of living in the moment.

He could rope anyone into his escapades, but one of his favorite victims was Vince, so he convinced him to explore a

Sedona trailhead that led to Indian Petroglyphs. They hiked up without incident but, not surprisingly, managed to get sidetracked and were soon running out of daylight.

They hurried to get down from the top of the plateau and somehow lost track of the trail. As they made their way back, blazing a new path, they had to shimmy down shale and grab hold of branches to stop themselves from falling about 200 feet to their ultimate death.

Vince went first and was able to find the trail and get back on track. Randy slid right behind him, but the branch broke, and he went over the cliff. Vince watched in horror, telling us Randy's normally squinty eyes were huge. Miraculously, Randy only fell about eight feet before catching another branch and saving himself. After Vince and Randy realized he was not going to die that day, they couldn't stop laughing and even made it home by dark.

On another trip, to Hawaii, Randy and Vince were hiking across the lava rock to see hot lava cascade to the ocean. It was about five miles but worth the hike.

As they were looking over the edge of a cliff, watching the flowing lava hit the sea, the wind turned. Suddenly, sulfuric acid steam from the lava flow hit them in the face. They almost fell in, not to mention they had to use all their drinking water to flush out their eyes. It was a miracle they survived to hike back those five miles, so very hot and thirsty.

When they got to the ranger station, which was about halfway to the car, the soda machine was broken. They made it to the car and planned to stop at the first place they could get anything to drink. This happened to be the Volcano winery. They arrived in time for a wine tasting. They thought it was the best wine they had ever had, and each bought a case. They were so excited to share a bottle with Pam and me, because it was so award-winningly good. Evidently, near-death experiences and extreme thirst affect your palette, because the wine was really terrible.

In Hawaii, the locals nicknamed Randy Papule, which means insane, reckless, wild, but fun, probably because he was fascinated with lava. As a geologist, this was understandable and might explain why, another time, he hiked to the flow and risked life and limb to roast marshmallows over lava with my brother, Geoff. He said the marshmallows tasted like sulfur, but he got some great video.

While hiking in Yellowstone National Park with Pam and Vince and their kids, we gave the children rigorous instructions: if they saw a bear, they were not to run but to stay very still.

One of their boys, Tom, was a few yards ahead of us on the trail when he came running back, screaming, "*Bear! Bear!!*" Sure enough, he had stumbled upon a bear and her cubs. We all started to run, knowing we just had to be faster than the slowest kid to survive, except for Randy, who stayed back and took pictures.

We had some crazy adventures, like whitewater rafting and sailing only to be caught by storms. If Randy saw a *No Trespassing* sign, he figured that wasn't meant for him, but rather for the uninformed public, to protect them from danger. He wasn't worried about meeting an angry landowner, because he knew he could talk his way out of the situation.

Randy learned to surf at age forty. He also tubed and waterskied. He competitively downhill skied, wrestled, and played football. However, he would never ride a motorcycle, because he thought they were too dangerous.

He would go anywhere or do anything in search of an adventure or in hopes of finding an alien. Once, driving from Abilene to Dallas, he followed what he knew was a flying saucer for thirty miles before it disappeared. The fact that it vanished proved it was, in fact, a flying saucer!

It really baffles my mind that he died of natural causes.

CHAPTER 12

Day 112 was Valentine's Day. I woke up, and after that first second it took me to remember, yet again, that he was dead, I realized it would be the first Valentine's Day in thirty years I did not get flowers.

Randy never got me candy, because, depending on what diet I was on, there was a good chance I wouldn't eat it. Sometimes, he did a lot more than give flowers. One year, he asked me to stay home from work, and he gave me clues and hints all day. A pair of gloves, the book *Love in the Time of Cholera*. He took me to breakfast and ordered for me, which was very odd behavior for him—previously unheard of. All day was full of different weird, inexplicable… stuff that became clear only that evening, as we watched the movie *Serendipity*. Throughout the day, he had acted out all the crucial scenes in the romantic film for me. It was amazing and very thoughtful.

When we were still in college, well before the digital age, he went to a photo booth and took about 100 sequential pictures of himself, mouthing the words "I love you." He spent hours making a flipbook, so I could watch him say in slow motion, "I love you" through photos, as my thumb flipped the pages of the handheld gift. It was the first of many simple, inexpensive presents that took a lot of his time to prepare. They have meant so much more to me than any jewelry he ever gave me.

I went to the cemetery, the last place I imagined I would be on Valentine's Day. I didn't find peace there or feel connected, but when I arrived back home, I received a flower delivery without a card. I assumed the flowers came from one of the lifeline ladies. No one confessed, but, once again, I realized how loved I was. Once again, I cried, because I had lost my love, and so many beautiful people felt like they needed to take care of me. I hated that.

The flowers were not my only present. I also found in my desk a CD from 2005 that said on the cover: *Happy Valentine's Day. Love, Randy.* He had made me a playlist of many love songs, and, serendipitously, I found it again on my first Valentine's Day without him. It was as if he had given it to me all over again. The songs on the playlist were:

1. "The Way You Look Tonight"
2. "You've Already Won Me Over"
3. "Your Body is a Wonderland"
4. "What Do You Get When You Fall in Love?"
5. "The Nearness of You"
6. "The Very Thought of You"
7. "Until the End of Time"
8. "You're My Reality, My Everything"
9. "How Much I Feel for You Baby"
10. "I Need Your Love"

I dreaded days like Valentine's Day and our anniversary, but the day after such a special occasion was usually worse. I prepared myself for the big occasion. I would think, "Wow, I managed to get through that, only to be blindsided the next day. That is what happened on Day 113. It was such a bad day.

I worked in Randy's closet all day, and I was functioning at a high level, trying to get done everything I had set out to do. I was acting, not allowing myself to feel.

When I finally sat down for a break, I saw on Facebook a beautiful tribute to Randy that a former employee and friend had posted, a montage of pictures of him with the music, "It Is Well with my Soul."

I was not prepared, and pain washed over me, horrible and constant. I did not have peace. It was not well with my soul. For days, there was no anesthesia and no sleep, no relief. I asked why and found no answer. I thought about numbing the pain with alcohol or some other substance, but in my core, I knew that was not a road I should go down; if it worked, I couldn't imagine stopping.

***

On Day 120, four months after he died, I wrote a letter to Randy.

> *Dear Randy,*
> *I don't understand why you left me. You knew how much I loved you, and you knew this is not what I would have wanted.*
> *My life without you is pain that is so extreme, some days I don't know if I will survive. Some days, I don't want to.*

You were more full of life than any other person I knew. I want to honor that and live without you, but I don't know how.

I knew I needed help. I couldn't go on the way I'd been going, and I couldn't figure out on my own what to do with this anguish. Consequently, despite a great deal of uncertainty, I joined a six-week grief recovery group sponsored by Hospice.

The very thought of Hospice made me envious. At least the people going into Hospice have some warning of their impending death. They have time to get their affairs in order and a chance to say goodbye. My envy was misplaced: There are no timely deaths, I have learned.

The leader of the recovery group was very kind and compassionate, as you would expect. Two other women in the group were in their late seventies, another point of irritation. I didn't question that they were grieving as much as I was, but I did resent the unfairness of their husbands living so much longer than mine. Another lady there was grieving for her mother, who obviously had lived to a ripe old age. There was one other woman my age who had lost her husband, too, and was feeling the tragedy every bit as much as I was. Her situation was worse, because she also had to deal with her own health problems and financial insecurity. I was overcome with compassion for her and so grateful I did not have to wonder how I would pay the rent or buy my prescriptions. An old adage resonated with me: If we all put our problems in a pile, would we want to pick someone else's or would we pick our own back up? I hated my own pile of problems but knew I would pick it back up, because it was familiar, and other people had it worse.

Every week, I dreaded going to the Hospice grief-recovery group, yet I looked forward to the class at the same time. The social worker suggested many books to read on surviving loss, and I was surprised that they helped. What helped most, though, was that they encouraged us to tell our stories. They prompted us with thought-provoking questions, and then they listened, wanting to hear about our loved ones, just as I wanted to hear about theirs.

One assignment was to do a storyboard about the person we were grieving. On the last day, we all shared our stories, and we all felt that we got to know one another's deceased loved ones. It brought me comfort to tell Randy's story.

It occurred to me that different people served a different purpose in my grief. My mother was someone I could stay mad at. She never did anything to warrant this sentiment, but she was a safe target for me to express my anger at my life. I could mistreat her and not answer her calls, and she was still always there. Pam was the person who allowed me to cry to her every night. I would cry, and she would listen to my tears, take care of me, and tell me how to take care of myself. Mandy took care of my business, when I could not. She opened my mail and paid my bills and did anything I needed her to; it was never too much. She understood that I needed someone to function for me and, sadly, she empathized. Candy was my encourager, the person who made me feel whole even though I wasn't. Geoff, her husband, made me feel like I had something to offer the world. Paul and Kathy were like an extended family who lived close by, the people I was always glad to see, the people who would move mountains for me, who understood so well what my family had lost.

Latimer was the one with whom I shared my loss of faith, knowing her faith was so strong my doubts would not hurt her. Though she had been through worse trauma than I, she had not lost her faith. Rebel reminded me I was still a mother, and how, even though my kids were nineteen and twenty-two, they still needed me. I also had a huge extended family on my side and Randy's side that grieved for me and with me. God... I wasn't sure what purpose God played in my grief, because I was still not speaking to Him.

* * *

Wesley's first year of college, Randy and I brought him and several friends to a cabin in Red River, New Mexico, so they could snowboard and ski. It was fun, once we got the plumbing to defrost so we could use the bathroom, a lot of fun. Randy snow-skied with the kids, and I stayed at the cabin, because I never liked getting cold. I cooked for the crowd, so food was hot and ready when they returned from the slopes, and then we played games or lit a bonfire and talked while roasting marshmallows. It was a trip full of huge inconveniences, but Randy and I took it in stride, though he with more stride than I.

This year was Wesley's sophomore year, and he wanted me to make the same trip with his friends. I couldn't imagine going without Randy, but I did want to let Wesley enjoy his spring break and figure out how to do life without his father and fellow adventurer. Mandy offered to go along, and so we went even though I was scared and uncomfortable.

During the day, while the kids did their thing, I cried and thought of Red River without Randy, and I hated it. On this trip, I had the fleeting thought of becoming a lesbian, because I could not imagine another man touching me, and I didn't want to spend the rest of my life alone. Mandy, a true friend, told me she would not judge me and love me no matter what I decided to do.

On the night before we left, the kids lit a bonfire. We all sat around in a circle, and the kids took turns telling one another what they liked about each other. They included me in their circle and expressed love and appreciation for me, as well as for Wesley. While I was by the fire, looking up at the stars and hearing these words of encouragement from all the young men and women not yet old enough to legally buy alcohol, I thought, "Life isn't so bad, and I can do this." I thought for the first time in months that maybe life was worth living.

But, the next day, the kids went back to college, and I faced the prospect of going to a house without Randy and had nothing left to look forward to. Once again, I was no longer okay with living, and was back to being okay with dying.

I was never suicidal, because I could never do that to my people. I did fantasize about getting struck by lightning or hit by a bus.

CHAPTER 13

Day 142: I wondered how many more days it would be before I stopped crying daily—or if I ever would. I was lying in bed, exhausted, after "crying yoga." During yoga, I had been enjoying fantasies of my throat being cut and my blood draining out. I knew this was very dark and I had to get some help, especially since my thoughts jumped from fantasy to planning a party to celebrate the Jewish holiday of Purim. (I still couldn't muster any desire to go to church or synagogue.) It was crazy, and I had to do something to make good come from this tragedy. For Randy, I needed to do more than survive.

My faith had always been a little odd. I grew up as a Reformed Jew in the suburbs of Chicago, fully embracing Judaism except when it was inconvenient—-and it was mostly inconvenient. Despite the inconvenience, I was a Bat Mitzvah, I knew a tiny bit of Hebrew, and I loved celebrating Jewish holidays, especially when it meant I could stay home from school.

Randy was a Southern Baptist with roots in West Texas and western Kansas. He did not know any Jews, just as I had never met any Southern Baptists. When we met, I immediately went about learning what Christianity was and what it meant to Randy, and he reciprocated, embracing all our strange traditions. My parents were so impressed with the way he took to lox and bagels and gefilte fish.

Our wedding in 1986 was officiated by both a minister and a rabbi. It was on the Fourth of July holiday weekend.

On Friday night, all our close family and friends gathered at a park for a picnic on the shore of Lake Michigan, to eat and watch the fireworks, a fantastic celebration that the City of Chicago graciously put on for us.

Saturday was the rehearsal and dinner and a lot of chaos. Randy realized at the rehearsal that he had forgotten his dress clothes at my parents' house, about forty minutes away. My stepfather Dave was sent to get them from the front closet, but during this chore, his adored indoor cat got out and ran away. Since he had to notify animal control and look for the cat, he never came back with the clothes, and Randy ended up wearing some clothes of his dad's to avoid going to the rehearsal dinner in shorts and a T-shirt. It makes me cringe thinking back on how upset I was that he didn't have the right clothes. Really what difference did it make? Tragedy has a way of making you realize what is essential in life.

At the dinner, we all packed into an iconic Italian restaurant, Fanny's, and there were many toasts and blessings. What I would have given to have had them recorded! In fact, what I would have given to have kept a diary or journal.

Randy was my diary and the journal to my life. Neither of us had the best memory, but together we remembered what we needed to. I might recall what was said in a conversation, and he remembered the longitude and latitude where it took place. He remembered faces, and I remembered names. I remembered what someone wore and how she wore her hair, and he remembered what music was playing. So, when I lost Randy, I lost part of my life history. Only my perspective of events is left to pass on and tell to our future generations.

After the rehearsal dinner, I remember walking with Randy to the hotel and our pledging our love to each other; our little private ceremony meant as much to us as the public one we had the next day. We vowed never to talk about divorce or even joke about it. After we got back from our walk, Randy and the groomsmen headed to Rush Street for the bachelor party.

I had to be at the beauty shop very early the next morning to get my hair and makeup done, so while Randy was drinking and carousing with the guys, I was in the hotel room with my mom, laying things out for the big day. Hose and bra, and something old, something new, something borrowed, and something blue—all there.

When we delicately pulled the wedding dress out of the bridal-store bag, we discovered that the many-layered tulle slip for under the dress's skirt was not there. I tried on the dress without the slip, but it looked like a negligée. There was no way I was wearing that. The Kansas ladies talked of staying up all night and sewing a slip for me from the hotel curtains, which had worked for Scarlett O'Hara, but did not seem very promising for me.

I was growing hysterical and began crying because my wedding would be ruined, but my mother saved it by remembering the name of the manager of the bridal shop. By now it was 11 PM on Saturday night, but she called 411 and got the manager's home phone number, which, remarkably, was listed. Mom called her, and she agreed to open the shop and get the slip, so, at midnight, we went to Michigan Avenue to pick up the rest of my wedding dress. Except for when my younger brother, Geoff, a groomsman, fainted during the ceremony because his collar was too tight, the wedding proceeded as planned. The wedding pictures made it clear that Randy and I both had stayed up way too late the night before, though it was for very different reasons.

Even with all glitches, the wedding ceremony and reception were magical. All the people in the world who mattered to us the most were there. There was so much laughter, and I was living completely in the moment. One tradition the groom and half of the guests were not familiar with was for the groom and the father of the bride to dance the kazatsky. This could be described as Russian breakdancing, where the two men hold hands, squat, and kick repeatedly until one of them gives up. It is fun to have the groom do this many times with brothers, uncles, guests, and anyone who wants to make him feel special. And boy, did Randy feel special. By the time we finished the wedding, changed into street clothes, and my brother drove us to the hotel for our wedding night, we were exhausted.

Randy was in a lot of pain, and though he didn't tell me he was suffering, our wedding night was not the kind of romantic fantasy all brides anticipate. The next morning, we got on a cruise ship for a four-day trip to the Bahamas. Once we were at sea, he confessed that he was really hurting on his right side, below his belly button.

We went to the ship's doctor to make sure he was all right, and the doctor turned out to be extremely hot—in a sexy rather than feverish sort of way. I was too mesmerized by him for a newly married woman. For the rest of the trip, Randy teased me about everything being a medical emergency, so I could look at Dr. Hot-as-Hell. He was worried about Randy's appendix and didn't want it to rupture, so he made arrangements for us to get off the ship to go to the hospital to get tested.

A liaison from the cruise line picked us up and drove us to the hospital; it was too dangerous to take a taxi because of all the drug dealers. The doctor was expecting us, but before examining Randy, they demanded all our spending money for the honeymoon—$100 cash, which was a lot of money back then. We waited for the test results with all the islanders who regularly spent the afternoon in the hospital, watching soap operas, because it was one of the few places on the island with air conditioning.

Randy, it turned out, did not have appendicitis, so we didn't have to get an emergency transport to Miami. The elderly, not-so-good-looking doctor told us Randy had probably pulled a muscle, and that was causing all the pain. He loved to tell people he pulled his groin muscle on our honeymoon, but we both knew it was from the kazatsky.

In our life together, just as at our wedding, we embraced both church and synagogue, gleaming gems from each. In my life alone, I had quit going to places of worship because I didn't feel like worshipping, and I thought, why should I go if it makes me cry? I was doing enough of that already. On the few occasions when I had gone to church or synagogue, no one talked about Randy, evidently assuming that any mention of him would make me sad. But I was already sad; not talking about him made me mad. In subtle ways, the parishioners let me know I was expected to smile and pretend all was well, because I would see him again one day. Why, I wanted to know, were there testimonies of people being healed and not any testimonies of them not being healed? Surely that was more common. Questions like that, though, made everyone around me uncomfortable. There was no help there for my spiritual problems. Strangely, I did feel that God loved me, but I was furious with Him all the same and didn't want to talk to Him.

I missed the Jewish holiday celebrations, so I figured I would do religion at home for a while. I asked some of my lifelines to come for Purim. Most of them didn't know what Purim was, but they dressed up and ate and drank with me and read the whole Megillah and laughed. Purim with friends was a small step forward.

I seemed to manage one step forward after every two steps back. Shock and denial seem designed to limit our pain to what we can handle. The problem is that, as it wears off, the emotional pain becomes more acute. On the plus side, the fog in my mind was starting to clear, and my thoughts were becoming more rational. On the down side, the sorrow was getting worse.

CHAPTER 14

On Day 160, I woke up and there was a dead rat on the living room floor. Strudel, probably had brought it in through the dog door, as a gift to show me how much he loved me; I did not feel loved but felt terrified. I had toughened up over the last five months or so and was no longer afraid of being alone, of death, of pain, or of driving long distances. I remained petrified of rodents, dead or alive. I guessed watching the 1971 horror film, *Willard*, about killer rats was too much at the age of seven. My fear was especially ridiculous because, in college, one of my jobs had been tagging live mice for the biological survey. Once, I spent the day in the lab, putting little earrings on live mice, only to come home to see a mouse scamper across the kitchen floor, and, before I knew it, I was on top of the table, screaming.

So, my fear was irrational, but knowing it was irrational didn't help. Now I was faced with a rat no less horrifying because it was dead and no danger to me. It was more than my strained, traumatized heart could handle, so I called a neighbor to get rid of it. This act of cowardice was actually pretty typical behavior for me.

Strudel frequently brought me dead birds and other carnage as he tried to earn my undying affection. I called Paden, Justin's best friend, to clean up a particularly grisly crime scene. When I called David, our former minister, to clean up the dead bird carcass that had been left in my bed, he rang the bell wearing a Superman costume complete with rubber gloves. On yet another occasion, I called my lawyer, who happily rid the living room of a beheaded bird.

The worst and most traumatic rodent encounter began with a scratching sound in the kitchen. I assumed it was Strudel, trapped in a cabinet or the pantry. I got up to go look, only to see Strudel sauntering by me. My adrenal gland went into overdrive, and my heart rate accelerated, but I continued into the kitchen to investigate.

Trembling, I opened the cabinet door to see… a rat, in my mind, huge and terrifying, and on the point of leaping at me. I slammed the cabinet door, ran back into the living room, and jumped on the couch. From there, I called the last person who had said to me, "If there's anything I can ever do for you, don't hesitate to call."

Steve responded quickly, arriving armed with a tennis racquet. He very awkwardly and humorously trapped the rat in a garbage can and took it outside, while I looked on in horror from the safety of standing on the couch. As extremely grateful as I was for all the friends who had come to my rescue, each time it was like pulling a scab off a wound. *Randy, this is your job*, I thought.

* * *

The horrible side effects of grief coupled with managing Randy's company and managing the business of his death was agonizing, exacerbated by my lack of sleep. I took sleeping pills, but they made me feel groggy the next day. I installed blackout shades and played soft music, but still I would lie awake for hours ruminating on should-haves and could-haves. Too often, when I did fall asleep, I had nightmares that woke me up.

Because I didn't get much sleep and often didn't feel confident doing Randy's jobs, I began to resent anyone I had to deal with in a professional setting. The worst new job was dealing with the life insurance company. I sat at Randy's desk and again called the life insurance company, only to be told I still had to wait for payment.

Because the Justice of Peace had approved an autopsy request that listed the cause of death as unknown, the insurance company would not pay on the policy without an investigation of whether Randy had died of natural causes. I wanted to see the autopsy report, and I dreaded the answer. Would it finally convince me my feelings of guilt were unwarranted? Or would it just make them worse? By pushing the company, was I trying to profit off my husband's death?

I needed the money for bills, after using my savings to pay for the funeral and autopsy. I was not keeping the investment properties rented as fully as Randy had, because that required effort and motivation I didn't have. Wesley was still in college. Juggling money to pay bills was a struggle, but wouldn't I rather struggle? Besides, the proceeds wouldn't be as much as they might have been, because we lowered the value when the premiums increased.

All these questions were moot, of course. It had been over five months. I hadn't received a check, and it didn't look as if I was going to any time soon. So I thought as I walked out to the mailbox in the bitter cold, but there in the box was the envelope from the Tarrant County Medical Examiner. I stared at it. Should I be with someone when I read it, or should I be alone?

I sat and asked myself what Randy would do—a pointless question. I realized the irony in that thought and opened the envelope. Though I had taken biology and chemistry in college and was a faithful watcher of medical dramas, I had no idea what the information actually meant. It did, however, say I could call the doctor who had performed the autopsy for more details. I called, and she was surprisingly accommodating and kind, perhaps because she had so much practice dealing with other people's pain.

She told me she was sorry for my loss. That by itself was a surprise. So often, in conducting the business of death, I had to say to people, "My husband died." Seldom had any of them responded appropriately or with any compassion. No, "I'm sorry for your loss." No, "That sucks." No simple kindness or even acknowledgement of the tragedy of losing someone.

This doctor was different. She told me in plain English that Randy had died of an enlarged heart that caused half of his heart to stop working. Probably his heart had begun to enlarge as many as ten years earlier, possibly as the result of an infection that settled in his heart, but there was no way of knowing. It would have taken very specialized tests to detect the problem, and the only cure would have been a heart transplant. Maybe all the pain in his legs and hips and the three surgeries had contributed to him dying when he did, but if he had not died on October 26, he would have died soon enough.

The scientific evidence of the inevitability of Randy's death should have made me feel better, and that night I did sleep for four uninterrupted hours. Despite that apparent improvement, though, I was back to wailing, something I thought I had put behind me for good, but I was wrong. I asked God, to whom I was not speaking, "Why?" And I heard, "Why not?"

***

I was still paying for Randy's phone, and I thought about canceling the service, but like everything, it would be an ordeal, since the account was in Randy's name. Instead of starting that process, I read all his text messages going back to 2011. They were so mundane. How I longed for a return of the mundanity of our life together!

People had stopped bringing food a couple months earlier, and I had eaten all the food in the freezer. When they were bringing it, I'd wanted them to stop, because there was so much. Now that it was gone, I was living mostly on pizza and cookies, except on those rare occasions when I got to cook for someone else.

I was very rarely hungry, but I ate anyway, not caring what crap I ingested or didn't ingest. That was not like me—not like the before me. I wanted to make a positive change, so I stopped for Thai food on my way home from work, knowing I had nothing at home but chips and salsa. Eating well is choosing life, and I hadn't been to the healthy Thai place since Randy died. I placed my order to go, and the straightforward owner said in her thick accent, "You don't look right. What's wrong with you?"

I told her I was sad because my husband died.

She gave me a long look. "Today?" she asked.

I couldn't help but laugh. No matter how good her food was, I would not have stopped for carry-out on the day Randy died.

* * *

I had to get blood work done to renew my thyroid prescription. I really didn't care about my thyroid, but I had enough problems with emotional outbursts and difficulty sleeping without my thyroid levels being out of whack. They weighed me at the doctor's office, and I was shocked at how much weight I had gained. Wasn't a person supposed to lose weight when they were grieving?

In a very sick way, I looked forward to the call that would tell me my blood work showed I had an incurable illness. When the call came, though, everything was within normal limits. I was very disappointed. Looking at myself, I wondered: Had I always looked this awful? Or did I see myself through Randy's eyes: a young, beautiful eighteen-year-old?

CHAPTER 15

Day 163. I didn't cry, which made the day monumental. It gave me hope, opening the possibility that my life would get back to some kind of routine. It also made me feel guilty. And when a friend called to invite me to a party. I did not understand how she thought I could go to a party when I had a dead husband.

It was at a party that Randy and I had the only serious fight we ever had. It was not long after we were married. The party was outside at our apartment complex, and there were probably 100 people there. Both of us were drinking and moving around the crowd separately, talking to different people, when I bummed a cigarette off someone. When I was in high school, I had smoked cigarettes for about a year during my rebellious period. And after that, every once in a while, when I drank, I had a cigarette. I don't know why—it wasn't a habit with me.

Randy hated smoking even more passionately than most nonsmokers did. Both his parents smoked, so he grew up with second-hand smoke. Ironically, his smoker parents told him not to smoke and even offered him $1000 if he still hadn't smoked by the time he turned twenty-one. He never did, not even a puff.

I knew all of this, but, at the party that night, I bummed the cigarette anyway, not really thinking anything of it. Randy saw me and crossed the distance between us with an anger in his eyes I had never seen before. Matter-of-factly, excruciatingly, he said, "You need to choose between cigarettes and me. I will not be married to a smoker."

My first thought was, *You can't tell me what to do*. My second thought was, *He is not kidding*, and I put out the cigarette, never to pick one up again. Randy loved me, I knew, but as much as he loved me, he had his standards. When he saw me with the cigarette, he had a split second to make a crucial decision, and he didn't hesitate. I never regretted the one and only time I was submissive in our marriage and the only time he'd asked me to be.

Funny, now that he was gone, I could take up smoking, and no one would care. I didn't. Instead, I started cussing like a sailor, which was something else he hated. He never used profanity himself, so I gave it up out of respect for him, though he never asked me to. Now, cussing was an act of remembrance. I think about Randy every time I do it.

Randy was not a saint. I thank God he was not, because St. Randy would never have had anything to do with me. He was honorable and brilliant. If I had to describe him in one word, it would be simple, but I know that would be misunderstood. Randy was a complicated person, but he saw the world and its many problems in black and white. He was pure in his faith and his love for others. It was a simplicity you usually see in children and in canines. There was that kind of delight even in the way he greeted me. I can't remember a time when I walked into the room and his eyes did not light up and he did not smile at me.

It really sucked that even the loss of how he had looked at me could be so painful.

His obituary listed the many occupations and careers he had, both successful and unsuccessful. I should have skipped all that, even though he was quite successful in the Air Force and in business. When I think about Randy's life, I never think about the jobs he held. What I think about are his relationships and his view of the world.

In his obituary, I should have listed *treasure hunter* as his occupation. As I've mentioned before, he'd started using a metal detector as a boy, running over the ground for hours, as he listened for the beeping to start. He brought his usual intensity to treasure-hunting. As he got older, he upgraded to better and better metal detectors, his thoughts of finding buried treasure growing more and more elaborate. He reveled in the family lore his grandfather had passed down to him and, several times, he went to look for a treasure he was convinced his great-grandfather had buried. Now I have inherited all the coins and arrowheads and other random prizes he dug up over the years.

His treasure-hunting skills went well beyond the search for metal junk. He could find treasure in people, too, and had no reluctance about digging for it. He instilled in our children the conviction that their interests and talents and dreams were treasures to be explored and excavated.

For instance, one morning, when Wesley was about three, he woke up talking about fish. He loved different kinds of exotic fish, and usually he and Randy were content to spend long periods looking at the ones in Randy's huge salt-water aquarium. On this morning, however, Wesley was talking not just about fish, but about whales, too, so within the hour, we were packing the car in preparation for driving 250 miles to Sea World. Why? Because Wesley was curious.

Justin loved building and planning and fixing, and as a child spent hours creating a game called Warhammer. Randy would drive hours to find a particular piece Justin needed to complete a village, so Justin would not become discouraged. Randy saw greatness in his children but did not care if they were great. He saw brilliance, but did not care what college or occupation they chose. What mattered to him was their personal fulfillment, so, whatever their current passion might be, he would go to great lengths to help them. What he wanted for them—all he wanted for them—was to be happy, moral, and living life to the fullest.

Time was a concept Randy never mastered, unless he was the one person who truly understood it. Countless times, we would be on our way somewhere, and because he had to take the road less traveled, we would be late. Once, we actually followed a rainbow, looking for the pot of gold at the end of it. A man with a less rambling spirit might have pulled over to take a picture of the rainbow, but Randy drove and drove until it disappeared, as rainbows always do. He had that sense that whatever he had to do, he had to do it *now*. He was, sadly and wisely, correct.

I had often joked with him, saying that, when he grew old and senile, I would make a big sandbox in the backyard and give him a metal detector. He could dig up the same treasure day after day, and he would be happy. In hindsight, the joke is on me, and it is a cruel joke, because he never had the opportunity to grow old or senile. While he was with us, he found the same wonderful treasure day after day in his family. Fearless, he would do whatever it took to help us find our potential, and for him it was all fun and adventure. He always encouraged me to write and take photographs. He sniffed out wealth in our teenage sons and their friends. He was a master at having good, clean, if somewhat risky fun, but always taking right and wrong very seriously, and the teenagers became what he saw in them when they were around him.

CHAPTER 16

I don't know if my friends made a schedule or it happened randomly, but it seemed like everyone had a day of the week to take care of me, based on their work schedule and other obligations. That was why it was unusual to have two of them at my house at the same time.

They both just stopped by because they "were in the neighborhood," and we were all sitting at the kitchen table, visiting. Innocently enough and familiar enough, one of the ladies started complaining about her husband and the fact that he didn't text her back immediately, when she texted him. The other one agreed and said how annoying it was.

I just stared at them for a second and then said, "My husband never texts me back, because he's dead."

They both looked ashamed, and I did not want to intentionally hurt them; it just came out like most everything did these days, without a filter. At that moment, I knew my new purpose in life should not be rescuing animals. Couples and families needed to be reminded to appreciate each other. We never know what our last words to each other might be. If I could somehow teach others to be kinder and more intentional in their relationships... And something else I could do was help people who had experienced horrible trauma to understand what was happening to their brains and bodies; then they would realize what they needed to do to help themselves heal. They could recover sooner and with fewer symptoms of trauma.

These were thoughts not a plan. I didn't have one of those until I went to lunch with Patty, a friend I'd always liked and had known for seventeen years—ever since our kids were in the same nursery school. We didn't spend much time together, because she was out of town a lot working as an attorney and a mediator. She also was a professor at Abilene Christian University, where she taught conflict resolution for families.

This intrigued me; maybe I could take her course or audit it. I could use the knowledge to help others communicate more peacefully, so they never had to regret their last words. She encouraged me not just to take her class, but also to go back to graduate school and get a master's certificate in dispute resolution. I could be a mediator. It was an ambitious plan for someone who was still as screwed up as I was, but knew I would have to try. And, honestly, I had nothing else to do.

* * *

It was the end of March 2014 and time for the annual Girls' Cruise. Aunt Norma had refused to let me cancel, telling me to wait and see how I felt when the time came. When it did, I still did not want to go, because I knew it would be tough on me and I would probably ruin the trip for the rest of them. Unfortunately, the usual excuses failed me. I was in pain anywhere in the world. I could go away and never come back if I wanted. So, I went and the cruise lived up to my pessimistic expectations.

On the first day of the cruise, I lost my credit card and had to cancel it. My purse strap broke. The luggage was lost. The very destination of the cruise was a problem: we were going to the Bahamas, the same destination as the honeymoon I had gone on with my kazatsky-impaired husband.

The second day at sea, my sister-in-law told a woman she met on the ship that this was a girls' trip, and we had all left our husbands at home.

I was so mad and hurt, I said, "I *didn't* leave my husband at home. Mine is dead." Again, no filter. Grief had left me without one, at least for then. I made my sister-in-law feel bad when she meant no unkindness at all.

On the third day at sea, I sat watching all the couples and thinking about how bleak my life was and would always be. I went back to the cabin, where I noticed how the bags under my eyes gave me a haunted look. I felt haunted. I spent the rest of the day wishing I had not come on the cruise. It was too soon for me to be good company. My heart was broken and couldn't be unbroken just by traveling to the Caribbean.

On the fourth day, we reached St. Thomas. At Emerald Beach, I found myself surprisingly happy, swimming in the ocean. It lasted until I got out of the water. My back started itching, leading me to thoughts about having no one to scratch it. I cried the rest of the day at the sadness of it, ultimately crying myself to sleep. I dreamed I was with Randy and there was still time to take him to the doctor to save him. I explained to him that he was going to die unless we got help. He went to the car to get something and started to run, moving impressively fast—running, skipping, leaping over obstacles. I was so impressed that it took me awhile to realize he was running to get away, so he wouldn't have to go to the doctor. It was a recurring dream.

On the fifth day, I met a woman who also had lost her husband. She was from Michigan and about my own age. We really, really talked about our losses. It was a gift. Sharing with someone who understood helped make me tolerable to those who didn't. I became able to participate more fully in the rest of the cruise. I went to the shows and got out of the room more.

On the sixth day, I realized the only place I was truly at peace was in the ocean. I loved the beach, and it really was healing to get some sun and to swim. I decided the word to describe how I felt being in paradise was *brutiful*, a cross between brutal and beautiful. Sometimes, as I swam farther out, I would think about intentionally drowning, but I always came back in. Another plus was getting to spend several hours with Randy's mom telling her how much I loved him. I do not know why that comforted me, but it did.

On the last day, I found myself ready to go home, though I knew, once I was there, I would want to leave again. An ice storm caused the last leg of our flight to be cancelled, and we got stuck at DFW airport, but I made hotel reservations by the airport and we Ubered there to stay safe until the storm passed. I was taking care of Aunt Norma, who told me that she did not know what she would have done if I had not traveled with her. It cheered me somewhat. I was glad I could help someone.

I made it home, and, as I had expected, horrible pain once again enveloped me. At home, alone, no Randy there to greet me, I realized yet again that he was never coming back. I missed him too much for it to be true, but there it was. I started to cry loudly, and Farfalle, my Labradoodle, stood up on her hind legs to hug me with her front paws. Taller than I was, she kissed me and licked away my tears, and all I could do was say, "Thank you."

Farfalle was my emotional service dog without the paperwork.

CHAPTER 17

I had begun to think about the future, at least in a hypothetical way. I could take another photography class, grow my hair long and let it gray, become a hippie and maybe join the Peace Corps, if it would have me. (This might well have been my life, if I hadn't met Randy.) All this thinking about the future was a good sign, I thought, a sign that I was healing.

One sign of healing I had not experienced: I had not been able to listen to music since Randy died, because I associated music so strongly with him. Randy loved music and was an accomplished musician. He played the trumpet at a professional level and, in college, won the Rocky Mountain Jazz Festival best trumpet player award. He played professionally for weddings and funerals. Eventually, he gave up his professional aspirations when he realized he either needed to put more time into it, to become the next Maynard Ferguson—his musical hero—or quit. He quit, and I don't think he regretted it because of all the time it opened up for him.

He did not ever stop loving music and listened to all kinds of it all the time. He stayed current and seemed to know every artist, both old and contemporary. He was great at playing

Name That Tune in just a few notes. I always teased him about being able to remember songs but could not remember people's names, though he was really good with faces. He could hear a song on the radio and, a few days later, pick it out on the piano playing by ear. Every Sunday morning, he would sit at the piano and play old hymns while the rest of us got dressed for church. I missed the music.

Randy had instilled both his love for music and his musical ability in our kids, and I wanted to keep that up, knowing the more they played the piano or trumpet or the more they went country dancing, the better they would feel. One of my favorite concerts of all time had been seeing Simon and Garfunkel on tour in 1983, and so for Christmas, I bought the boys and me tickets to hear Paul Simon in Houston. I found the experience bittersweet. Every song reminded me of Randy, but I did realize how much I missed music and how healing it could be despite the pain.

Paul Simon singing "Bridge Over Troubled Water" delivered a sucker-punch. The boys had lost their dad and best friend; I determined they shouldn't have to face the loss of me as well—or at least what was left of me. I could not replace their father, with his enthusiasm or example of living, no matter how well I managed to be as a mother. As young men starting out in the world, they needed Randy. I wished I had died instead of him, for their sake. For Randy's sake, I am grateful to have spared him the pain of losing me that I had been experiencing in losing him. In a weird, twisted way, it seems I had taken a bullet for him, even though he was the one who was slain.

Not only did my children not have their dad to talk to about their love lives, but I also don't have their dad to talk to about their love lives. It had been one of my favorite topics of conversation. While I wondered if every girl one of the boys dated would be The One, Randy took it all in stride, confident that one day they would find their soul mates.

Wesley had been in love with Maddie for over a year, and I took great comfort knowing Randy had gotten to meet Maddie and her family. She is kind, smart, beautiful, and always a lot of fun.

Oddly enough, I really fell in love with her at Randy's funeral, where she sat on the floor in front of the church with the rest of the kids. Wesley sat in the pew on one side of me with Justin on the other. During the service, all the kids were facing forward, paying attention to the kind words David and Sam had to say about Randy and to the video of Randy and our family that Paul made. All the kids were facing forward except Maddie, who didn't look forward but backward, her attention constantly on Wesley. Her face wore such an expression of concern and compassion as she willed him to be okay. I saw in her face how much she loved him, and I was relieved Wesley had her in his life. I knew she would help him recover.

I was more concerned for Justin because, just a few months before Randy died, he and his college girlfriend had broken up. Not only that, he left behind his close-knit group of friends when he moved to Houston, a huge city totally unlike the city he had grown up in. He had the stress of juggling a new, demanding engineering job with a highly competitive graduate school. And now, the father he adored and frequently emulated would no longer be there for him.

When Justin had first moved to Houston, I told Randy how worried I was about our son and all the challenges. (It turned out he was dating and making new friends and excelling at school and work—I was just the last to know.)

Randy just smiled and said I should not fret, that Justin would meet someone who would be the true love of his life. He was confident that Kara was out there, and he was right, though he never got to know Kara. I regret that. The way kind, smart, and beautiful Kara looks at Justin is the way I looked at Randy, and it makes my heart happy Justin has found the love he deserves.

On the way home from Houston and the Paul Simon concert, I tried to think of what I was thankful for, though every source of gratitude that occurred to me seemed to be accompanied by a genuine thought of what I had lost. Still, I wrote down the only thing I could think of: that I was grateful for my memories. Then I wrote about how my neck hurt and was stiff. This reminded me how Randy would rub my neck, especially when we were on road trips. He would drive with his left hand and, with his right hand, rub the tension out of my neck. I was horrible at reciprocating, and now I felt guilty about that.

I should have given him more neck and back rubs.

CHAPTER 18

It seemed incredible that six months had gone by, and I had to face Easter. It had always been a delightful time for us. When the kids were little, their cousins on Randy's side would come to town, and they would all hunt Easter eggs together. As the kids got older and we all got busier, we started celebrating Easter with our close friends. We started a new tradition of adult Easter egg hunts. Randy and Paul made treasure hunts, hiding eggs stuffed with cash instead of candy.

Consequently, none of us had ever lost interest in the silly tradition of Easter-egg hunts—until this year. I didn't know if I should invite the Walkers and Taylors as usual or instead pretend the holiday no longer existed, which was my preference.

We carried on, so to speak. We cooked and ate, and then, when it was time to hide the eggs, Paul did it solo. It made him cry, and we all wished we had just dropped the tradition of the adult Easter egg hunt. How do you choose between two choices when both are wrong?

On big occasions like Easter, Randy was conspicuously absent, but even on typical, insignificant days, his absence seemed unreal to me. I remained in denial on many levels.

Frequently, I would think of something I needed to tell him or I would wonder what he was doing, and I would be blindsided once again by the loss of him. At night, I thought about him despite every effort to distract myself, so to get any sleep, I continued to take sleeping pills.

The sleeping pills usually took about thirty minutes to take effect, which gave me time to consider random memories of Randy, such as his love for iced tea. When he was young, he drank a lot of Coke. Then, in adulthood, he switched to Diet Coke. In 1991, before Justin was born, he went to Big Bend to camp and hike, and he experienced the wild beauty of the region and the unavailability of Diet Coke. Consequently, he decided it was a good time to give it up, and he switched to iced tea.

From that time on, he never went anywhere without his quart container of iced tea and knew which convenience stores sold the best. On our early visits to Illinois, when he would order tea, the server would assume he meant hot tea, the concept of iced tea being evidently foreign to the Windy City. He was motivated to change this, and whenever he could, he encouraged store clerks and restauranteurs to carry iced tea. Over the years, iced tea become easy to acquire in Chicago, and Randy was convinced it was solely because of his determination. It was a frequent claim of his that he brought iced tea to the area. Randy drank a lot of iced tea, I reflected—a lot of liquid, in fact—and, drowsily I wondered if it had been responsible for his enlarged heart. With that uncomfortable twist in my thoughts, I fell asleep.

Though showering and going through Randy's stuff remained a challenge, I began to contemplate even more challenging goals I could pursue. Photography—I could do something with that. Or I could climb Wheeler Peak, the mountain in New Mexico Randy and I had talked about tackling after Randy's hip replacements. Or I could write a book about grief that told the truth, something that seemed to be needed. The sense of calling that continued to grow in me was the possibility of helping families to resolve conflict before it was too late. If people could realize how awful they would feel at the death of their spouse, maybe they would be more intentional about treating that spouse with love and respect while they could. Patty and I could develop a program to coach couples contemplating divorce on how to communicate successfully. We could work with them on listening more and talking less, while seeing the perspective of their "enemy." Pursuing that calling would mean going to graduate school, so I began to contemplate that prospect more seriously.

The day came when I awoke feeling like jumping another hurdle. Why not go to breakfast by myself? Though I had been to restaurants solo many times in my life, thinking nothing of it, it had become a massive thing, because now it was not by choice, but because my restaurant date was dead.

I felt hopeful, believing I could do this thing. Where should I go? I didn't have to ask Randy where he wanted to go… Wow, that hurt. I went anyway. Sitting at the next table over was an old man who was also dining alone. On the basis of no evidence whatsoever, I assumed he was a widower and that this was one of many meals he ate alone each week—just like me. I thought about talking to him, showing him some kindness by being social, but I didn't. Though I wanted to, when it came down to it, I didn't have the gumption.

After breakfast, I went home and was sitting outside in our spot on the porch where we liked to drink coffee and I began to think about going to a movie. I hadn't been to one since Randy's death. Maybe I should call someone to go with me—maybe I could ask the mailman who was dropping the mail in the box. Instead of following through, I went by myself and gained inspiration from *Unbroken*. Eating by myself and going to a movie alone all in one day was a massive accomplishment for me, and it made me feel proud and horrible simultaneously.

* * *

The beginning of May had always been one of my favorite times of the year, because we got to celebrate Justin's birthday, my birthday, and Mother's Day all in the same week. I was trying to decide whether this year I was up to all that celebrating when I realized that my dogs, Farfalle and Bagel, were missing. Evidently, they had crawled through the fence after digging a hole.

Farfalle was always getting in trouble, often because she loved to eat anything and everything—the patio furniture cushions, the leather couch, and even a pair of scissors. She ate a shofar—a ram's horn blown as a wind instrument—that decorated the mantle, though I couldn't blame her for that one, because technically a shofar is a bone. Whenever I reported her bad behavior to my friends and family, they would be horrified and beg me to get her trained, but I knew I didn't have the energy to be consistent. Besides, I hated my stuff and wanted it to all go away. What difference would it make if she ruined it?

Candy came over, and we took her car to search for the missing dogs. We found the puppies across a busy road a couple miles away. Though I was glad to have them home, honestly, I think Candy was more relieved than I was. She evidently thought, if I had lost the dogs I loved and who were my constant companions, it would devastate me. For my part, I was as low as I could go emotionally. I thought, I could always get more dogs.

I ultimately decided to ask the kids to meet me for the weekend of Mother's Day and found a condo to rent at Lake Conroe. It had a pool and was close to both Wesley and Justin. I also asked Kelsey and Bryce. Kelsey was my friend Rebel's daughter and Wesley's best friend, and she was like family.

In the end, only Justin and Kelsey could make it. Still, it was a welcome distraction. Justin and I celebrated our first birthdays without Randy.

Randy and I decided early in our marriage not to get each other presents for birthdays, because I hated shopping and he never knew what I wanted. We bought our own gifts, though we did give each other cards to acknowledge that we were worth celebrating. Going through his stuff after he was gone, I found every card he ever received from me, the kids, and our other relatives. These cards meant a lot to him, and I hoped everyone knew it.

When Randy turned thirty-eight, a lot of friends were having fortieth birthday celebrations. I decided I could really surprise him if I went ahead and had the party two years early, and it worked. He was so surprised that he was extremely late to his own party. Our good friend was supposed to take him to explore a ranch and then deliver him at precisely 7 PM to our house, but they didn't make it. When I questioned them about why they were so late, neither one had a good explanation, just that they were having fun.

At this party, Wesley was three, Justin was six, and they both thought it was great fun to surprise their daddy. I wore a red sequin shirt, and I remember Wesley telling me how beautiful I looked. In his three-year-old eyes, I probably looked like a Christmas decoration: what could be more beautiful, except maybe Santa himself? In reality, Randy was the beautiful one, the smart one, the talented one, and the fun one. I don't say this to diminish my worth—it's just simply the truth. I believed I married up. The crazy part of the story, though, is he honestly thought I was the beautiful one, the smart one, talented one, and the fun one. I guess it was true love on both sides.

The theme of the party was maps. Randy loved maps, and all the guests were instructed to bring a map for a present, which has left me with a bunch of maps I don't know what to do with.

As much as he loved maps, Randy loved technology more. When GPS came out, he had many hilarious conversations with the OnStar representative. He would push the button on the dashboard, and when the voice would reply, "Hello, Mr. Polk. How can I help you?" Randy would say, "Call me Randy," and then go on to ask some asinine question like, "I was just wondering, who invented ice cream?" Randy used OnStar like people currently use Siri, and the OnStar reps would laugh with him, never appearing annoyed, because Randy really was delightful. Later, when we moved on to Garmin, he loved to get directions in different languages. His favorite was Swahili, and he could do a perfect imitation of the different dialects he'd learned from Garmin. Fortunately, he rarely actually needed the directions; he was testing Garmin. He always said, "If you don't care where you are going, any road will get you there."

When geocaching became the fad, Randy was all in. It was the perfect entertainment for him. He could satisfy his treasure-hunting bug and use his mapping skills and, best of all, waste hours at a time with the credible excuse of playing a game. He had the opportunity to geocache in Europe, Israel, and many places in America. Once, in Switzerland, the clues brought us to a private dairy farm, where Randy did his best to explain to the landowner, who knew a small bit of English, why we wanted to traipse around his farm. The landowner never could understand exactly what we were there for, but he did let us do our traipsing all the same. He did understand that we were American, so he let us know that he bought all his bull semen from Wisconsin.

Randy was a great children's birthday party enthusiast. I would do all the planning, but he made them fun. When Justin was six, Randy had taken him to see the graphic adventure film, *Dante's Peak,* about a volcano exploding and the aftermath. The movie was highly inappropriate for a six-year-old, and it made an impression. Justin had to have a volcano birthday party. Randy made an exploding, papier-mâché volcano for the kids, and the backyard became hot lava.

Another year, he filled the sandbox with treasures, and the kids treasure-hunted. When we had a food-fight party—which was exciting—we learned the hard way that mustard burns the eyes. When we had a party at the lake house, the lake flooded, and we were stranded with ten boys for a few days, until the water receded. We couldn't get on the lake, but we sat on the roof and watched debris float by like it was the best movie of the year.

For my thirty-sixth birthday, Randy wanted to do something special for me, because it had been such a tough year. I was the lifeline to a dear friend whose husband was dying of cancer she could do nothing about. After her loss, I was a witness to her pain. As hard as that was for me, it did make me a better wife. Watching her love and care for him through his cancer made me more deliberate about showing Randy my love. After watching her lose her dear husband, I could not take my own husband for granted. The first fourteen years of our marriage were great, but ironically, because of her loss, the last thirteen years were even better.

Anyway, for my birthday, Randy decided to surprise me with a weekend away, just the two of us. I was working full time and had two small children and a husband, and I was grieving with and for my friend. Randy was worried about me having a breakdown of some sort, he said, and my life was intense and stressful. The only person it seemed that I wasn't taking care of was *me*.

Surprising me with a weekend away was no small job. Randy had no idea which dresses I might want to wear, so he packed all the dresses in my entire closet. He packed all the clean clothes from the laundry basket, because he thought I must wear those often. He packed everything in my bathroom in a box, not knowing exactly what I would need. He arranged for the kids to be taken care of. Then he picked me up from work and said, "Surprise! I am taking you to the Mansion on Turtle Creek in Dallas for your birthday."

All the preparations he made were impressive because Randy wasn't a planner. On the first night we arrived, a masseuse came to our room, to give us a couple's massage. Pampered as I had never been pampered, I began to relax. Randy bought tickets to a play the next night, and we had dinner reservations at a gourmet restaurant. When we got back to the hotel, we went to the bar for a nightcap. It was crowded, but no one was sitting at any of the tables in a section of the bar that was roped off, so we went around the rope and sat down at a little table for two. The waiter came and asked us for our drink order.

As we sat sipping our perfectly shaken martinis, John Travolta and some of his entourage walked in and sat down next to us, giving us a nod and saying hello. Evidently, he assumed he was supposed to know us, because we had a table in the private section he had reserved. Maybe we were investors in the movie he was in town to promote or something. Who knows what he thought? After a few minutes, he came over and said hello and sat down with us. An onlooker from the other side of the rope sent him over a bottle of wine, and he smiled and mouthed his thanks, but he didn't get up.

Cleverly, having heard on the radio that Olivia Newton-John was in town for a breast-cancer fundraiser, I said, "Did you know Olivia Newton-John is in town, too? You should call her." *Grease* had been a favorite movie of mine, when I was a teenager, and of course I had loved, *Welcome Back Kotter.*

After John went back to his own table, possibly to ask his cronies who the heck were those people, we left quickly, not wanting to spoil the night by being found out.

CHAPTER 19

After the birthday/Mother's Day weekend with Justin and Kelsey, I knew I had to choose between life and a living death. This purgatory of in-between was not working for me. I finally made a phone call asking for help. The call was to Trish, the nurse practitioner I had been going to for my sleeping pills and my thyroid prescription. She had always been so compassionate, and I did not know where else to turn. To my surprise, she asked if she could come to my house the next morning for coffee.

When she arrived, she said that she felt I needed to tackle my grief holistically. It wasn't only a physical problem, although it was manifesting in many physiological ways. It wasn't only emotional, even though I was indeed depressed. And it was not only spiritual, although I was having a crisis of faith. She sat at my kitchen table and took notes on a legal pad. She wrote down two pages of symptoms, from crying to lack of motivation to insomnia to anger. She told me she would get back with me, and she left.

Two days later, she called to ask if she could again make a house call and come over for coffee. Her insight was that, for me to get well, to get beyond my depression, I would have to tackle all my issues simultaneously, because they were all connected. She made it clear she was not advocating that I get over Randy, just that I manage my grief in a healthier way. She recommended a therapist but told me a therapist alone wasn't going to solve my problems. If I did not also exercise to increase my dopamine, serotonin, oxytocin, and endorphins, talk therapy would not be very effective. If I continued to eat crap, my immune system would not help but hurt me. She gave me a nutritional plan with a lot of organic fruits and vegetables; she recommended that I started boxing and gave me Annie's number. Boxing, she said, would give me much needed exercise and an outlet for my anger.

The most important thing I needed was to get more sleep, so she increased my sleeping pill dosage. Meditate every day, she suggested. Practice aromatherapy. Take up something artistic or creative. One thing I had managed to do right on my own was to arrange weekly massages, thanks to Angie, because physical touch was so important. The real reason I had survived to this point was my extensive support network—my community, my tribe. Everything was connected, which was why I had to make changes in all areas of my life, if I was going to feel better. I knew that I would follow this long list of suggestions precisely because I was at the end of my rope. I could no longer stand the misery

I called the boxing instructor, Annie, and admitted I was scared to join her class—not only because I did not think I could handle the physicality of it, but also because I cried a lot without notice, which made me uncomfortable being in public with strangers. She invited me to come for a private session, and, before I knew it, I was boxing and kickboxing five days a week. I was not good at it, but the loud, mostly angry, heavy metal music, combined with my sweat and my tears and Annie's willingness to listen to me talk every day about how much I missed Randy, all contributed to my healing. The more my muscles hurt, the less my broken heart hurt.

I called the therapist Trish had recommended, JoAnn, and she was so kind over the phone. She told me how sorry she was for my loss and said she would like to try to help me. I was so scared to see her, afraid of what my actual diagnosis might be, but I did. Looking back, I realize what a genius she was.

In the first few sessions, I barely spoke, just sat there staring at her and crying. The only time I became animated, instead of having little or no affect, was when I talked about Randy. My first homework assignment was to listen on CD to a favorite storyteller of hers. I listened and became a fan and slowly looked forward to hearing the next story. She was working to get me interested in other things—anything besides my pain, and it worked. I told her I needed to figure out who I was without Randy, and we worked on that. I took personality tests.

Eventually, we talked about how much I had depended on Randy for my social life. Yes, I had some remarkable friends, but he was the outgoing one, the one who was comfortable in new social situations. She encouraged me to do what Randy had done, things I had never had to do because he was there to lean on. Talk to strangers, she said, just for practice.

I did for the first time when I was on a crowded train. Instead of looking around enviously at all the couples, I told myself, "The next person who gets on this train, I will talk to, whether man, woman, or child." My guinea pig turned out to be a pudgy, middle-aged man with kind eyes and wearing a uniform. I looked him in the eye and asked him how was his day going? He looked back at me and smiled like I had made his day. We chatted until the next stop, when I had to get off. I can still see him, my first new friend after I'd decided to live, even though we were only friends for a couple of minutes. I don't remember his name, but he made a difference to me, and I did to him.

Again on Trish's instructions, I got a nutritionist—Amy—and cut out all chemicals in my diet that might hinder the natural production of my feel-good chemicals. It was easier than I thought to do what Amy told me. I just followed her meal plans. It was freeing, not having to make decisions, and the cooking didn't bother me because I had always enjoyed that. I replaced the sugar and carbs in my diet with fruits and vegetables and found myself free of the cravings. I felt better, and the better I felt physically, the better I felt emotionally.

I was not yet ready to pray or go back to either of my previous religions, but I still had the Gathering. Back in 1996, I had joined a group of women who changed my outlook on life. These women got together once a week on Tuesday nights to pray. It was outside of my comfort zone, and I was the youngest by five to twenty years, but the women were fun, and I needed friends.

Randy had just resigned from the Air Force, and our built-in friend group had left for their next duty station. We were the only ones who had stayed in Abilene, mostly because we didn't have anywhere else to go. I didn't want to go back to Chicago, because of the weather, the cost of living, and the traffic. I also didn't want to go to Western Kansas, because it was too rural for me. We never really got around to picking a better place to live than Abilene, and for so many reasons, I am glad.

Anyway, the women in the Gathering were all world-changers. They included a colonel in the Army, a nurse, a social worker, teachers, stay-at-home moms, ranch owners, artists, and a local politician. They were all ministering to someone somehow. They were single, divorced, widowed, and married. They were black and white and in between. They belonged to churches of different denominations and believed different theologies, but they were all ministering to someone in some way, individually and together. They showed me and taught me about unconditional love, when I did not know I needed it.

We would meet at Maria's warm and welcoming old house. She is the kindest combination of angel and twisted sense of humor you would ever want to hang out with. One year, she made me a Christmas wreath out of tampons and maxi pads. After my hysterectomy, she made me a cake shaped like a uterus. Other than myself, she was the last person to see Randy conscious. Another member of the Gathering wrote poems and sent them to us from Afghanistan. Another showed me how to love someone who had hurt you so much they didn't deserve it. She showed her ex-husband love and respect, even though he had been very publicly unfaithful. She remained a friend to him for the sake of their children. Another member showed me how to survive during financial and emotional adversity, after her husband totally abandoned her and her child. Another showed and taught me how to love strangers by loving the downtrodden. Yet another showed me what it was like to be a faithful public servant.

The Gathering always celebrated birthdays with a potluck dinner, a cake, and a card for the special lady. Sometimes we griped that we didn't pray enough and talked too much. Sometimes we griped that we prayed too much and talked too little. These women loved Randy and loved me and over the years they suffered with me and grieved with me and laughed with me and helped me to return to joy by showing me that helping others was a way of helping ourselves.

I was very fortunate to have been part of this group for many years before my tragic personal crisis. I knew, if I had looked for the group after my tragedy, it would have been too late.

I started thinking about that. What happened to all the women who needed a Gathering, but when trauma struck, they had nowhere to turn? I added this problem and how to solve it to my new purpose-for-my-life list. Even during my darkest hours, I never gave up going to my Gathering. Mostly, I sat and cried, and for many, many weeks, they just sat and cried with me. Eventually, I was able to sit and listen and not cry, but still I did not pray. I was too angry.

When Trish gave me my prescription to find a spiritual outlet, though, I knew I already had the Gathering. I began to focus on the prayers I heard my soul sisters sharing and to silently agree. I no longer made the Gathering all about me and my problems, I opened myself to the other genuine problems out there.

I started having birthday parties at my house again. I have never met a group of women who, over some wine and comfort food, could move so quickly from a holy moment to the subject of anal bleaching. These are the women who carried me, and whom I have carried. These are the witnesses to my life. These are the women who prayed for me until I was able to pray again.

CHAPTER 20

In June of 2104, Justin asked me what travel destination his dad had always wanted to visit but had never been able to go. I immediately thought of Machu Picchu, the Incan citadel in Peru. Justin said, "We should go there for Dad." I loved the idea of us living for Randy instead of dying for him.

Even though it was six months away, we started planning a trip for the end of December 2014; the only time Justin and Wesley would have time off from school. This was another new purpose for me, so I did my research. I knew, if Justin and Wesley were going to enjoy the trip, then adventure had to be the theme—and, at the moment, I lacked the stamina to hike to Machu Picchu and trek through the Amazon rainforest. So, I started training for the pilgrimage with my boys.

I was training to hike for miles through two feet of mud and trek up to the top of Machu Picchu, starting at an elevation of 11,152. Though I knew I wouldn't be able to hike the Inca Trail, I did not want to hold the guys back any more than I had to. I started listening to books as I walked my dogs. The combination of being outside and having my mind occupied made me look forward to the walks.

With Annie, I pushed myself to do more squats, to climb higher on the incline, and to box the punching bag harder and harder until my hands hurt. It helped that, with every punch, I delivered a stinging rebuke. With my right hook, Randy, why did you leave me? With a cross, God why is this happening to me? With each jab, I gave the punching bag my problems of the day, one after the other. I cried and cursed and I wondered how I was going to survive another day, another week, a lifetime. Annie encouraged me to let it out. Afterward, I told her one story after another about my life with Randy until she felt like she really knew him. This, along with my therapy with Joann, was an integral part of my healing.

I tended to think about how Randy would have handled his loss, if I had been the one who died first. At first, I was grateful he was the one who left me—not because I had any will to live, but to spare him the pain I was enduring. No one should have to experience that, certainly not Randy. After the first few weeks, as my life lost all direction and the pain got worse instead of better, I began to think about how he would have handled the loss better. He was a radiant and joyful person most of the time, better at finding things to do and losing himself in work or play or whatever. He would have been better equipped. I vacillated between the ridiculous thought that I was glad to take this one for our team, willing to suffer the loss of us, and the thought that it would have been better for me to die because he would have recovered better, faster. It was all mind games, because, obviously, I hadn't had a choice in the matter.

* * *

In the thirty years I knew Randy, I remember him getting mad three times. This does not count various mild irritations I often caused him—changing my mind at the last minute about where I wanted to eat, after he had his taste buds set for another place; talking while he was trying to watch something on television. When I talked, he would pause the program, look at me, and wait for me to finish. It was also unusual for us to go somewhere new and not fight about directions and the best route to take. For the record, he was always right. Well, not *always* right, but always right about navigation.

The first time I really saw his rare temper was in 1984, while he was in graduate school and I was an undergrad. He was working for a company selling trips to Daytona Beach for spring break.

He filled two charter buses with students from the University of Kansas and made the arrangements for a twenty-four-hour road trip. He reserved twenty rooms at a hotel on the beach in Daytona with four kids to a room. Each bus carried a beer keg and forty students, not the best recipe for a smooth trip. The kids started puking due to the beer, and the bathroom on the buses quickly quit working. Still, we were young and resilient, and we made it to Daytona Beach.

Randy went into the hotel to get the room keys, thinking to group everyone with their preselected roommates and give everyone directions to their rooms. We discovered that Florida law prevented evicting anyone from their motel room when their rental expired, even if their room was reserved by someone else. In other words, there is no such thing as mandatory check-out dates.

This was a problem, because we were arriving on the last day of Daytona Beach Bike Week, the second-largest motorcycle event in the country. 500,000 bikers were there ahead of us, and they weren't leaving. Hopefully, the hotel manager told us, there will be rooms tomorrow. Of the twenty rooms reserved, only three were available. Sorry, but it was Randy's problem.

Randy dealt with it. He assigned all the boys to one room and all the girls to another. The third he reserved for himself, as a place to answer questions and handle complaints. Surprisingly, the kids were pretty cool with our predicament, happy just to get off of the bus and have a place to store their stuff and shower before they went to sleep on the beach.

In the chaos surrounding our arrival, Randy asked me to get his stuff off the bus along with my own. I dragged the suitcases off and waited with the rest of the KU Jayhawks for direction as the bus pulled away to pick up more students in Minnesota.

After a couple of hours, we finally made it upstairs. Randy realized his camera bag was not with his suitcase and asked me where his camera was. He told me it was in the compartment above the seat, and I had to break the news that I'd forgotten it. It was an expensive camera, and you might expect that that was the moment he lost his temper, but it wasn't. He was very understanding. He called the travel company to ask the bus driver to locate his camera and keep track of it for the two days before the bus was due to return to Daytona.

The company representative was very rude, making a reference to the stupid girlfriend who had left the camera on the bus. That was when Randy lost it. He shouted that his girlfriend was not stupid, that if the company had done what it had promised to do, none of this would have happened. As I listened to him defend me, even though he was under a considerable amount of stress and it was an expensive camera, I knew that I was in love with him and wanted to marry him.

The next time I saw him lose his temper was about ten years later. At that point, we owned a retail store, and Randy had just separated from the Air Force. A customer parked in front and came in to transact his business. When he went out, in full view of our floor-to-ceiling windows, he threw a dirty diaper down in our parking lot and drove away.

Randy hated litter, and he hated how disrespectful some people were of other people's property. So, he went outside, and picked up that dirty diaper, and put it in a plastic sack. Then my love put the plastic sack in a padded manila envelope and mailed it to the customer at the address on file, along with a note stating he had forgotten something. Did Randy break any federal laws by mailing that envelope? I did not ask.

The last time he got mad was when I asked him to move a big forty-by-sixty-inch painting that was hanging over his aquarium. He said it would be hard to get to the painting without moving the fish tank, and he couldn't do that. "Try," I pleaded.

Randy got a ladder, climbed onto it, and reached across the aquarium, trying to get a grip on the big picture from three feet away. The painting slipped and fell into the tank and the frame and glass broke. He cussed, which was something he never did, and that was the beginning of the end of his salt-water aquarium hobby. He didn't have the energy to set up another tank to transfer the fish to while he cleaned the first one and reestablished the necessary ecological balance. Instead, he gave away his fish to other collectors. He got angry on that occasion, but he got over it. His ability to not sweat the small stuff was inspirational to me—mainly because we never know what the next day will bring.

CHAPTER 21

On the last day of June, I woke up and went through my usual routine of assessing myself based on how much I had slept. I was okay. Sleeping badly was never an excuse to skip the gym, but this was massage day, the one day of the week I didn't go.

Angie would be coming with her table, her friendship, and relaxing touch. Randy had been her client—before his death, I had only gotten the occasional massage—but her nurturing friendship now provided me a safe place. I would usually lie on the massage table she dragged to my house so I didn't have to go out, and cry.

I went to the back room to feed the dogs before Angie arrived and I found my beloved Bagel lying in her open crate, motionless. Dead. I went to the couch and sat down. I was numb. Why did the people and animals in my life die without warning?

Angie let herself in, as she always did. "What is wrong?" she demanded. I told her Bagel was dead. "No way!" She went to the back room and confirmed that Bagel was in fact dead.

"Had she been sick? Acting funny?" All I could do was shake my head.

Ultimately, we took Bagel to the vet to do whatever they did with dead pets. I was sad and shocked, I still miss her sweet company, but I am here to tell you it was not like losing a family member. I imagine the only people who say that and mean it are people who have never actually lost a family member, at least not a close one. When I read on social media that losing a pet is similar to losing a child, I say a prayer that the author of the post would never learn the difference.

Still, this latest trauma caused me to reassess my relationships. It was easy to sort out the people who helped me from those that hurt me. There were both types in my life, and they made for a startling dichotomy, very yin-and-yangish.

Some well-meaning friends and family members had absolutely let me down when I needed them the most. One friend in particular, I had seen a couple times a week for years before Randy died. She hadn't called me since the week after Randy, her friend and my husband, died. Probably it was too painful for her.

I certainly knew what it was like to be the witness to someone else's pain. It is horrible, but to shrink from it is selfish. If you don't have the answers, and most likely you won't, then you can still be there, saying, I don't know what to say. In my own experience, I remember very little of what most people said, but I do remember who showed up and who didn't.

A relative told me that enough is enough, Randy was in heaven now, and I needed to just get better. I didn't know there was a deadline for grief, but I guess there was in her manual. When she said that, I had to make a decision that our relationship was more important than the offensive attitude, which was hard—and her words hurt me—but I am grateful that grief and trauma did not claim our relationship as another casualty that day.

For all the people who let me down, I continue to be amazed at the number of people who stepped up to support me. One woman whom I certainly knew and thought of as a friend, though not in my inner circle, texted me every day for a year with the simple message, "Thoughts and prayers." Another woman with whom I had worked with twenty years earlier and seen a couple times a year at best called me weekly for months, until I agreed to see her. She just wanted to give me a hug.

One young woman, who had only been to my house a couple times as part of a group of kids, turned out to be a gifted artist and presented me with a breathtaking painting of Randy, an abstract with many colors, but also totally recognizable as Randy. It took her almost a year to create it.

Justin also created a brilliant gift for me, taking everyone's comforting comments from Facebook to make a three-dimensional canvas that looked like a sunset with all the quotes on it. I still am not sure how he did it, but I know it helped him as well as me.

Maddie painted a beautiful original piece of art done with many colors that she said was a view of heaven she had seen in a dream. All these gifts served as a tangible, daily reminder that I was loved, and Randy was loved.

In general, the people who tried to help me could only address one part of my pain. They concentrated on the physical, emotional, or spiritual, but with the exception of Trish, not many could address a combination of these. I was lucky because I had a community, and each member in it had a role, so that eventually all of me was taken care of.

What I experienced after Randy's death, in addition to horrible grief, was post-traumatic stress disorder, and my symptoms included difficulty sleeping, difficulty concentrating, easily startled, irritability, anger, agitation, and hypervigilance. Sometimes, my feelings were numbed, and sometimes I was emotional and hypersensitive. Unwanted memories intruded on my thoughts, and I had nightmares and flashbacks. My physical symptoms included unexplained bruising all over my body and difficulty catching my breath. The more people I told that I was having a crisis of faith, the more friends I lost. Some even judged that my lack of belief was the cause of Randy not being healed.

CHAPTER 22

I was tired of people spouting platitudes to try to make me feel better when in fact they made me feel much worse. The platitude I hated the most was, "God needed another angel." If I was having a good day, I would smile and nod my head. If I was having a bad day, I would say, "How the hell do you know what God needed?"

After ten months, I accepted the fact that I would have to take control of my own life and grieve the way I needed to grieve. I would spend more time with people who gave me strength and limit my relationships with people who stole my energy. If people were tired of me talking about Randy, if it made them uncomfortable, I would write about him, and they could choose if and when they read my stories.

By now, my grief was capricious. It was like the nagging lower-back pain that's always there, but you are so used to it, you don't think about it, until you lift the thirty-pound bag of dog food the wrong way, and the searing physical pain hits you. Not to mention, the emotional pain when I think Randy should be lifting this for me. My grief was always there, nagging and persistent.

Then there is a trigger, like watching the parade on the 4th of July and not celebrating our twenty-eighth wedding anniversary. And later, I try to brace myself for the searing pain, but it's too late. The silent screams start, and tears are pounding to come out, and my breath is stolen, and I can't get a deep breath. I pray this intense grief ends and I can go back to the dull ache. I know the sooner I surrender to this wave, the faster it will be over. Sometimes, it lasts a few moments, and sometimes, a few weeks. The grief always wins, and the gut-wrenching sobs take over.

I have learned the sooner I get to the punching bag, the quicker I will recover, because the familiar physical pain is so much easier than the emotional pain. Before the latest wave abates, I think about all I've lost. Then comes the evil whispers of should-haves and could-haves.

As I recovered from my PTSD and my brain fog cleared, the natural anesthesia of confusion and shock began to wear off, and my grief surged with a vengeance. There was a difference between trauma and grief, I was learning. I wanted to recover from the trauma, but the grief, as agonizing as it was, led me to think of Randy. I feared I couldn't stop grieving without thinking of Randy less, and I didn't want that.

In August, I decided to go on a trip to Italy with an eclectic group. Pam, whose son was working there for the summer, her father, her mother-in-law, and my two sons. I had been to Europe once before, when Randy and I went to visit Justin while he was studying there.

As with everything post-Randy, this was bittersweet. I got to spend time with my best friend and my kids, but I also thought a lot about the last time I had been to Europe with my travel mate.

In general, it was a great experience, and keeping up with the travel agenda helped me to regain some of my lost energy. Pam's mother-in-law, who had lost her husband a couple years earlier, gave me some great advice that I took to heart: Men would be interested in me, because they know I was a good wife and they want someone to take care of them. She said, "You do not get in a relationship to take care of someone else. Learn to take care of yourself, and that will be enough."

Since, I couldn't imagine being in a relationship with anyone, what she said made sense. I was on my own, if unwillingly, so I should embrace the gifts of not being accountable to anyone, of going anywhere I wanted to anytime I wanted to go, of eating what I wanted and going to bed when I wanted and buying what I wanted. I could change careers or do nothing. I could make money or live very simply and not worry about money.

My biggest challenge was knowing what I wanted, because the symptoms of grief were always in the way. Physically, I was on track. I was eating healthily and boxing for exercise, and I was starting to see the rewards: sleeping better, if only because of physical exhaustion, and taking comfort in a routine. Emotionally, I was still a wreck and felt like I needed to do something with my life or die.

* * *

I decided I needed to do something to commemorate the one-year anniversary of Randy's death, an event to give his friends and family the opportunity to come and talk about him, if they wanted to. Talking had certainly helped me, but the family discouraged me from planning this memorial event, because they said it would be too hard on me. They would not participate.

I decided I wanted to be with my sons on the anniversary of their father's death, so I went to see them. The five-hour drive gave me plenty of time to second-guess myself. I didn't know what we needed to do. There was no instruction manual. I wanted my sons to talk, but if I said, "We should talk about what you are feeling," they would shut down.

Wesley said he wanted to spend time in nature, because Randy would have liked that, so we planned a hike. Justin wanted us to eat Randy's favorite foods, so we planned a stop at Whataburger. My contribution was inspired by the songs I heard on the radio on the way down to meet them, songs that reached me through the airwaves and then through my grief filter. I asked Justin and Wesley to make a playlist. It would simply be called Randy's Playlist.

Over the years, music has been a huge part of our lives, even though I personally couldn't carry a tune in a bucket, couldn't play any instruments, and had no rhythm. When we dirty danced in college or chaperoned middle school dances to make sure there was no hanky-panky going on, I depended on Randy for the music.

The most memorable and meaningful example of this was when he performed Louis Armstrong's version of "It's A Wonderful World," singing and playing the trumpet and sounding just like the original. From the small stage in front of our friends, he looked at me and pointed to me during the line, "They're really saying I love you." I was embarrassed by the attention. I wish now I could relive that moment and understand that it wasn't about me.

On this visit, I rented a motel room and had no trouble staying there by myself, which was a real sign of progress in my healing. When Justin and Wesley came over, I started talking about Randy's favorite songs. We thought about the times we heard him perform certain songs on the trumpet or piano.

I told them about all the concerts Randy and I had gone to over the years: Kansas, Chicago, ABBA and the symphony; from Michael Martin Murphey to Trans-Siberian Light Orchestra to Weird Al and everything in between. We had seen a disturbing Elton John in Vegas and a heartstring-pulling Pat Benatar.

So, Justin and Wesley and I spent the 366th day since our lives had changed so drastically never leaving my hotel room. We listened to hundreds of songs as we reminisced, picking out songs and discarding them as we made our list. We talked about Randy's favorite songs, and we remembered him singing them for us, or going to concerts with him to hear the songs, or cranking the tunes on the boat. We remembered him performing them on the trumpet and piano and certainly imitating the artists with his versatile voice. We added then threw out songs and made a list. Some of the songs made Randy's Playlist because they honored our grief and helped us heal. All of the lyrics had deep meaning for us.

It is my hope that, as family and friends listen to this very diverse collection of music, music almost as diverse as Randy himself, they will remember him and enjoy the music!

Randy's Playlist is:

1. "Spirit in the Sky"
2. "Fly Like an Eagle"
3. "Gonna Fly Now"
4. "Stairway to Heaven"
5. "Dream On"
6. "Sunshine of Your Love"
7. "High of 75"
8. "Pennies from Heaven"
9. "Wizards in Winter"
10. "Love is in the House"
11. "White and Nerdy"
12. "Represent"
13. "Over the Rainbow"
14. "I Hope You Dance"
15. "Bridge Over Troubled Water"
16. "Dust in the Wind"
17. "I Just Called to Say I loved You"
18. "What a Wonderful World"
19. "Farther Along"

That weekend with the boys had more healing than I could have prayed for and ended with eating green chili cheeseburgers from Whataburger and hiking. None of us really had an appetite, but we went through the motions. After it was over, I made the decision to host a celebration of Randy's life on what would have been his fifty-fourth birthday.

About a hundred people came to the house and stood around wherever they could. For over two hours they shared stories about Randy. The common theme: He was my best friend. When it was over, we gave everyone a CD with Randy's Playlist.

It did my heart good to be around so many people who loved Randy, who were willing to talk about him and listen to stories about him.

CHAPTER 23

It had been a long year, but I made it through the first anniversary of Randy's death and his birthday. Round two of the holiday season without Randy was coming, and I made the decision to go to a weekend-long intensive for grief at Gold Monarch Healing Center. I had been making progress, but I wanted more good days than bad.

The immersive weekend provided healing for the mind, body, and spirit, which I appreciated. It was confirmation that I was on the right track. Still, it was bittersweet in that I met others who had also lost their loved ones. And it was hard.

Two weeks after my healing retreat, my boys and I left on our long-scheduled pilgrimage to Machu Picchu. Our young guide, named Eric, and another couple from New York met us in Lima, Peru, and the six of us began our adventure together. Eric took care of me with such kindness that I might have been his mother. The couple from New York had a complicated relationship, but they were fun and funny, and we all bonded instantly.

The first night, as we walked around Lima together, I thought, this is great. I can do this. The next day, we took a small rowboat across the Amazon River after receiving strict instructions not to touch the water because of the poison dart frogs and piranhas and parasites. The experience was surreal: knowing I was about to have the most exciting adventure of my life, and I was about to have it because Randy had died. A black caiman slithered into the river, looking just like an alligator. I looked at my kids and found I had no words. It was another brutiful moment.

We were going to be cross-country skiing through the mud to get to our lodging in Peru's Amazon rain forest, so when we arrived on the opposite shore, we were fitted with boots up to our knees, to keep the mud out, and provided with ski poles and literally life-saving bug spray. As we traveled, everyone in the group was much faster than I was, but Eric stayed with me for the couple hours it took to trek in. Every few minutes, I was rewarded with seeing and hearing a red howler monkey or puffbird or gigantic lizard. It was the most physically challenging thing I had ever done, except maybe having a couple babies. With every grueling step, with each concrete step, I thought of the steps I had to take to get to these quicksand-like steps.

I made it. I got to our open-air, mosquito-netted, generator-powered lodge just in time to change for dinner. The lodge was charming, but for dinner I anticipated being served cuy (guinea pig) or anticuchos de corazon (grilled heart) or something else I had read about. I was pleasantly surprised that the food was both delicious and familiar.

Unfortunately, after dinner, I dropped my brand-new Leica camera in the toilet, which was more like an outhouse with a pit latrine than American plumbing. From that point on I was going to have to rely on my phone for pictures, which was disappointing, but there was absolutely nothing I could do but get ready for the next event, a night hike through the rainforest to see the creatures of the night.

It was fascinating. I got to know the woman from New York like a sister and found her to be another stepping-stone to healing. She was single without children and had devoted her life to her successful career.

As I told her my story, her comments made me change my perspective. She said, even though I did not get the time I wanted with Randy, I did have thirty years, and I had experienced the kind of love that most people never experience. Most people don't have grown children who like them and want to spend time with them. They don't have great memories and often have only regrets. These insights did not make my pain go away, but they did go a long way toward helping me not feel sorry for myself anymore.

Two days later, we had to cross the Amazon River in a metal canoe before trekking through the mud to Cusco and Machu Picchu. As soon as the six of us were in the boat, though, it started taking on water. We knew enough Spanish to understand that our non-English-speaking Peruvian rower wanted us to take up the small bucket and begin scooping out the water we were not supposed to touch, before the boat sank. I had a MacGyver moment and asked if anyone had a piece of gum. I chewed it as fast as I could and then used it to plug the leak. Amazingly, it worked, keeping the water out long enough for us to get to the other side of the river.

The next day, we took the train into Cusco to celebrate New Year's Eve before our next adventure. We all went to dinner and had a great time. I could not believe how much I was laughing. It was a significant change from the previous New Year.

My kids loved the thousands of people packed in the square, setting off fireworks and drinking and singing and dancing, but as midnight approached, I decided to go back to my room. Though I was much better than I'd been the previous New Year's, I couldn't face the prospect of feeling like I was supposed to kiss Randy and not being able to. Once back in the room, I cried and tried to think positively about another year without him.

From Cusco we took a train to Machu Picchu, where we boarded a bus to take us to the bottom of the ruins. After a tour of the ruins, Justin, Wesley, and I climbed to the top of the mountain, where we looked down over the ancient ruins, completely speechless.

I imagined Randy there, wanting to see every nook and cranny in the time allotted, taking pictures and videotaping and talking to strangers and laughing. We didn't do any of those things ourselves; we just stood silently with the tears running down our cheeks. To be there at the end of fourteen months without Randy seemed a surreal human accomplishment.

We wanted to leave something of Randy's at the top and finally settled on his Million-Miler card. Though the plastic card was now worthless, it meant so much to us symbolically. We were telling Randy that we would continue to live for him, no matter how many challenges confronted us, telling him thank you for making us adventurers.

As we looked up to the sky and down into the valley, we thought how much we missed him and would miss him for the rest of our lives.

EPILOGUE

Eight months after Machu Picchu, I did start graduate school, studying conflict resolution and communications. From my life experience and the lessons learned in school, my business partner and I developed a program for women post-trauma that has helped hundreds of women move forward after becoming victims of loss or violent crimes.

Also, I have fun helping couples communicate using the four tools that Patty and I developed. I don't pull any punches, as you might imagine, and my genuine, raw testimony of loss helps people to see just what life might be like, if their partner were gone. More often than not, this is what it takes to get people to choose their relationship over being right.

It took me two years to make up with God. But we are now closer than ever.

The second year indeed is the hardest.

Four years after Randy died, I made another lifetime commitment to the love of my second life. We are grateful for every moment we have together, because we both know the next moment is not guaranteed.

Even after seven years, I still cry sometimes.

THANK YOU

I wrote this book because I had to. It was part of my journey to more healing. My healing would not have been possible without the many friends and family who loved me when I did not act loveable. Some of you are mentioned in this book by name. The rest are in my thoughts.

Thank you for encouraging me to write more stories about Randy. I appreciate the invaluable help with editing, proofreading, technology, and many other tasks, Maria, Emery, Cayce, Neil, Candy, Nellie, Fran, Kathryn, and especially Mike. I am so grateful for your contribution to this labor of love.

Also, I would like to thank my parents and Randy's parents for making us the people we were and are. I would like to thank all my siblings and Randy's siblings for being there and being fun witnesses to our lives.

To my children and those who love my children, you make my life worth living, and you're fantastic humans.

To all the fellow grievers, my intention is that this will be a message of hope. I could not have had the courage and motivation I needed without you.

And to Tony, for giving me back laughter—the greatest gift.

SITE REFERENCE

Annie, boxing coach: @brickhouseboxingandbarbells

Chess: Justin@KnightSchool.com

Gold Monarch: GoldMonarchHealingCenter.com

Marla: www.marlakanepolk.com

New Beginnings: Newbeginningsbigcountry.org

Palm House: PalmHouseAbilene.org

Resolution Solutions: ResolutionSolutions.net

Trish, nurse practitioner: RestoreWellnessPrimaryCare.com

Tony: TonyBarkerMedia.com
   Tony, my life partner, is not referenced in the book because I did not know him during the first fourteen months after Randy's death. He and I wrote a song together, called "Thank You for Loving Her," available on Spotify, iTunes, and Apple Music

ABOUT THE AUTHOR

MARLA POLK is a communications coach specializing in helping those in broken relationships heal through communication tools she developed as a mediator. She is Managing Partner for Resolution Solutions, a conflict resolution consulting company. She is the President of the Board of Directors for a nonprofit, the Abilene Palm House, that mentors at-risk individuals and works specifically with women who have been survivors of violent crimes.

Marla is the mother of two grown, happily married sons and lives in Abilene, Texas with her two dogs, two cats, and devoted partner. Find her at www.marlakanepolk.com.

Made in the USA
Columbia, SC
28 November 2020